BLOOM

Queer Fiction, Art, Poetry, & More

VOLUME 4, ISSUE 1

SPRING 2012

BLOOM

ARTS IN BLOOM PROJECT, INC.
5482 WILSHIRE BLVD, #1616
LOS ANGELES, CA 90036
queerarts@gmail.com

EDITOR
Charles Flowers

POETRY EDITOR
Aaron Smith

FICTION EDITOR
Wesley Gibson

BLOOM is a publication of Arts in Bloom Project, Inc. a nonprofit organization dedicated to queer writers and artists and their audiences.

EDITORIAL POLICY

BLOOM does not discriminate against the imagination. Gardeners must identify as Queer (LGBT), but the flora of their labor need not serve any preconceived notion of beauty. Peonies, sweet williams, ragweed, and gladioli—every shape and shade of blossom—are all welcome. Let the garden grow.

For submission guidelines, visit our website:
www.artsinbloom.com
www.facebook.com/bloomliteraryjournal

ISSN 1550-3291

CONTENTS

POETRY

THANK YOU
FOR MAKING A RECENT
DONATION TO

BLOOM

Liz Ahl
Lucy Jane Bledsoe
Tom Healy
Charles Jensen
Michael Klein
Ed Madden
James Magruder
Peter McNamara
Peter Pereira
Jason Shultz
Stefen Styrsky
Eric Tran

If you'd like to make a donation to support BLOOM,
please contact Charles Flowers at queerarts@gmail.com,
or visit the website, www.artsinbloom.com.

BLOOM
Chapbook Winners

IN 2010, BLOOM held its first chapbook contest. The two winners are excerpted in the pages that follow, and both chapbooks are available for order at www.artsinbloom.com.

Judge Minnie Bruce Pratt had this to say about the poetry winner, *Bruised Gospels* by Phillip B. Williams:

"*Bruised Gospels* is poetry that saves, sanctifies, and celebrates the lives and bodies of Black men who make art and love with each other, for each other. These singing, ferocious poems 'fight against fate' and win."

Judge Richard McCann had this to say about the fiction winner, *A Small Uprising* by Alicia Shandra Holmes:

"Here is a story that goes after large themes through small and intimate gestures, a story that's as human and warm-hearted as it is well-made. 'A Small Uprising' achieves strong feeling through a language that's plain and direct and strongly felt. At the end, the resolution comes with a wonderful lightness of touch."

Curse 6 – Oil and Water

I don't question the rats
their quick strokes through fields,
through alleys. Something hidden
in an emptied can of soup, a beast
licking what's left from its lips. I don't judge
the rat its hunger, or the ecstatic cat
bounding in a vacant lot with a tail dangling
from its mouth. The dog with the loud
growl gets tossed old meat sooner
than the dog with the patient whine.
The shut mouth never gets fed. The agile
pounce at the right angle, never right
without practice. What hungers you
so that your knees replace your feet,
eyes so distant with desire you see
yourself coming quickly back around
for another taste before the first is had?
Behind my garage, two men sucking
wildly, knock over my garbage cans, and run
away from the sound of their hunger, the not-
yet-used-to echo of such hollow shame.

FROM *40 Curses and a Prayer*

ALICIA SHANDRA HOLMES

from "A Small Uprising"

Question on job application: *What would you do if you saw a coworker stealing? (a) Report theft to supervisor immediately. (b) Give coworker the chance to return what was stolen. (c) Wait until you and supervisor are alone and then report theft. (d) Nothing. It's none of your business.*

THE SKY FILLED SUDDENLY WITH SNOW — lightfalling at first then blizzarding down all night on the city. While I worked, I watched the storm through the all-glass front of the Speedy Mart. All down Woodward Avenue the stores and restaurants disappeared into the whiteness, everything blurred, indistinct. Each hour a plow rattled through the storm, unable to clear a path through the chaos of drifting snow. I was working a double until dawn because the midnight-shift worker hadn't shown up.

"Evening, ma'am," said Michael, a regular, as he walked in. He brushed snow from his coat and poured himself a cup of coffee. "Dangerous out there," he said, pausing for a moment as we watched the storm.

"But beautiful too," I said.

THAT NIGHT, 436 MILES FROM DETROIT, in a town too small for me, my mother was praying for me. She lived in a sturdy old house surrounded by pines, and her prayers had become as steady as her heartbeat or her breath.

It had begun a month before at St. Francis Hospital. When my mother learned she needed heart surgery, she heard the trumpet sound. You must pray without ceasing. And she did. That Sunday she got down on her knees and was born again again. She felt like white lilies, she said. I should've known then that the Spirit trumpeting through her would also disrupt my life.

She first called Jesus her Lord and Savior when I was five years old. We were baptized together — born again and sanctified. She felt like white roses, she said.

AFTER HER SURGERY, MY MOTHER lay unconscious three days. Her face seemed paler than the steady-falling snow. I stayed by her side, and when she woke, she started praying for me.

It had long been her conviction that I had the wrong job, so she started praying that I'd leave Speedy Mart. My cousin had been raped and beaten nearly to death while working at 7-11, and my mother feared this — or worse — would happen to me.

After surgery, though, she knew: God had brought her through and now would free me from my job. She would pray without ceasing until it was so.

I didn't pay much attention. I had no intention of leaving my job. But the Spirit is a mystery, and I don't think even she could have foreseen how her prayers would be answered.

THE STORM HAD ENDED BY THE TIME Sam, the Speedy Mart manager, arrived in the morning. "Go get some rest," he said.

I waded through the snow to my Matador, cursing myself for not bringing gloves. The entire car was covered. As I cleared off the car with a rolled-up newspaper I'd had in my backseat, my face and hands froze painful then numb.

I counted the red things I could see: streetlight, stopsign, restaurant awning.

Every winter I craved red. It usually began midwinter after weeks of snow and white-gray skies. But that year it was worse. I craved red all winter. I stained my lips blood red. I carried red apples with me which I'd eat throughout the day. I used red pillowcases. Yet I still craved more.

"For Christ's sake," said Sam, walking over with a shovel and an extra pair of gloves, "put these on." He used the shovel to knock most of the snow off my car.

"You're a saint," I said.

"Tell it to the church," he said and started shoveling the sidewalk.

To my relief, my car started. It'd been rattling with unsettling noises since I'd driven north. I vowed to see a mechanic as soon as I had some cash.

Romantic Comedy
Enchanted (2007, rated PG*)*

Goddamn the snow that sent me into the theater for two hours' refuge
in projected light. Even if I only wanted escape, goddamn my wanting.
Goddamn the romantic comedy, a genre pockmarked by selves
who never fulfill themselves. Goddamn the men holding hands
next to me in the dark, their snippets of growl gilding the film,
their delight at the comic heroine's transformation from cartoon to flesh.
She falls from Technicolor to Times Square, rising from the underground
in her marriage gown. Goddamn the heroine's flawless skin,
her eyes rinsed red from waking in a drainpipe at the beginning
of a soured century. And then, God, after the movie's over
and I've been flung into another city's sprawl, after I've been crowd-filtered,
released from the fold forlorn, damn the bride emerging
from the Renaissance Hotel across the salted avenue, a vision
in an unsullied dress. Goddamn the fabric that will be so luminous
in the portraits, it will loom from its frame, fill all onlookers with longing
to feel it in their mouths, bite it into shreds. Goddamn what's wrong with me,
I can't stop thinking about the fairytale princess, her optimism a gust
of perfumed wind in a flagging sail. As if no one is shipwrecked
on the shores of Love Always Fails Us. The groom is whispering
Goddamn you're wet in the broken laundry room in the hotel's basement
to a bridesmaid whose white fur wrap is a strip of fallen weather
on the cement floor. Goddamn all beauty made in betrayal.
Goddamn the bride, she wants to live the heroine's life, all shivering lip
and beaded veil, goddamn her until she is weeping, the cartoon fool.
The goddamn concierge opens the car door for her, bending elegantly
at the waist to palm her dress into the limousine. He fingers the slight hem.
Goddamn him, showing us what he could do to skin on the belly,
skin on the thigh, my untouched cheek. Goddamn the wind,
it isn't the hand of a lover. Goddamn the wineglass shattering inexplicably

at the best man's toast. The best men, the worst men, the extras in the movie
which brought me to tears—goddamn them and the gift of my body.
Goddamn the land and the air, the fish and the fowl, the light in the day
and the night in the night. But do not damn the lit cigarette I'm holding
too close to my face. Not it, God. Though it burns acrid
between my fingers, it does not leave me alone to lift my face up
out of the halo of darkness in the cold of Chicago.

—for Amber Dermont

CHERYL DUMESNIL

The Heart Has Four Chambers

The meditation leader asks us to see
what's in our hearts right now, and I question

when that muscled fist in my chest
became a place, four chambers like rooms

in the Morgan Library—lapis columns
and horse-hair stuffed walls dulling

midtown Manhattan's traffic cacophony.
Or the Catacombs of Paris, subterranean

hallways lined with precision-stacked
femurs, hollow skulls of the innocent

dead. Which brings me to the tunnel
my wife's brothers dug in a rented backyard,

big enough for five kids to crawl in and
eat butter sandwiches while their parents

filled the kitchen with cigarette smoke
and broken glass. We're lucky the roof

didn't collapse, she laughs. Maybe
it did, I think, trapping that rag doll girl

in her hand-me-down gingham frayed
at the hem. Meaning, part of us always

stays back, while the rest marches on.
Or maybe I'm the kid with mud-packed

lungs sleeping under the concrete patio
the next tenants laid. Maybe that's why

we recognized each other at first glance
that summer the reservoir held no water,

and those two girls jumped off
the dock's dark edge, and the night sky

proffered a handful of tinfoil stars.

CHERYL DUMESNIL

The Conception Myth

First of all, there's no turkey baster,
just this needleless syringe and a plastic

vial with a salmon-colored frozen chip
at the bottom, no bigger than the tip

of my pinky finger. The label promises
twenty-four-thousand swimmers will

emerge when the ice defrosts. We need
only one. And it seems easy, like that

carnival game where you shoot water
into the open clown mouth and a balloon

blooms out of its head. Until we watch
the movie where sperm spin like drunken

mole rats, bumping into fallopian walls
while the egg sits on her barstool sipping

her last-call vodka, checking her watch.
Post-insemination the bowl of my pelvis

warms like a room full of bodies and I
wonder if one, which one will wander

down that hallway, hear her whispering
behind the closed door, and knock.

AUSTIN BUNN

Curious Father

Y ES, HENRY WOULD LIKE to say something. In the early part of his marriage, Henry started an extension to the house that he never finished. Ten years and counting, conduit still sprouts from the ceiling. Pink ribs of insulation are just there. Margot, his wife, put in a twin bed to home it up. She was afraid their daughter Effie would go and electrocute herself, fork in socket, to a curly-haired cinder. But Effie didn't go in because she thought the room was haunted and, in a way, it was. Eventually, there was this unpainted door they didn't talk about and never went into.

One morning this spring, Margot opened it. This was right after the tests on her lump came back with nothing doing, and she was all about new patterns. Like soy milk, like no more unfinished business. When she moved the bed to clean, when Henry heard the crash of his magazines and videotapes, his body tensed in the magnifying quiet. At the state concert hall in New Brunswick, where he stage-manages, he's heard a soloist's violin crack and fold in from pressure. He's seen the lighting grid come raining.

Irrevocable things happen all the time.

Henry rose and went to her. Margot sat the mattress of the twin bed, leafing through his porn, his secret cache. Men in the photos, mouths and bodies penetrated on every page. At her feet, she'd made a neat stack of the videos, the sad lot of them, whose titles — Fuckbuds, Uncut Timber, Dungeon Cops II — gave Henry's shame a fresh edge.

"Sweetheart, tell me," Margot said, slipping her arm around him, "did these do you any good?" And at that moment when their marriage made no sense, when all they had were their patterns — the little sun of grapefruit in the morning, a joint each month on Date Night — Henry was more in love with her than he'd ever been. Love like she was the last log of a splintering raft. Henry was, is, terrified.

M ARGOT'S THERAPIST FAXES Henry's therapist a brochure. Dawn Manor, it reads: When it's time to get found. On the front, a group of men sling their arms over each other like a softball team. Honestly, Henry prefers a little more space between people. This Manor, a big Victorian in the Catskills, is a kind of workshop for "men who love men" but are bent out of shape about it. Henry can't find anybody close to his age in the photos, but he never sees people his age in advertisements unless it's for pills or Florida. On the last page, staged with professional light, two men with identical goatees knock their heads together with a golden retriever between them. "Dawn Manor is operated by author/certified intuitive Bodi Charles," the caption reads, "and life-partners Spike and dog Rigby."

"Life-partner," Henry says, and it depresses him. At fifty years old, six months out of his marriage, he's never had a partner or boyfriend or fuckbud and suspects he never will. Now that his secret life — furtive visits to an adult bookstore, terrified opportunism in public restrooms — has become his actual one, he sees he has chosen to die horny and alone.

Henry takes the brochure back to his apartment only to ignore it. Tonight, Van, the sound engineer at the concert hall, is coming over to "christen the escape pod." They've been friends for years, but lovers in Henry's mind for months. At work, the crew calls Van "the Pirate" on account of his hoop-earring, shoulder-length hair, and grizzle along the jaw; the nickname alone brings Henry's cheery erection out of early retirement. Van wears construction boots with the laces so loose they're really flip-flops. Everything he keeps on him — wallet, watch, Leatherman — is hitched to his belt with metal links. Van is twelve years younger, a divorced father whose son visits on weekends, but Henry is lonely enough not to care that he's in love with a straight man.

"I like the Christmas lights," Van says on arrival, taking in the studio. "Very bachelor Noël."

Van wears a sports coat inside out, pockets flapping like ears. You can just do that? Henry thinks. Van's longish hair tucks under a cap with "VOLUNTEER" stitched across it; this visit, it occurs to Henry, may be a form of community service. Under his arm, Van carries a radio with a crude tinfoil antennae and volume knob that "gets angry" if you play with it too much. "From my divorce to yours," Van says as he leans back in the other chair.

"Beer?" Henry asks.

Van shakes his head. "Soda? I'm sober these days."

When Henry hired him, Van had been a mess. In middle of his own separation, Van showed up at work with blood-shot eyes and lazy about feedback. Henry sensed around him a general state of transition, and he felt compelled to know it, join it, as if he himself were there, choosing his life all over again. Early on, Van's car got repo'd — a negotiation in the settlement had gone sour — and for over a month, Henry picked him up and drove him home, an errand that became the high point of his days and made work seem like the interruption. He'd never met someone so open. Van was fearless and unencumbered, lobbing provocations out from the passenger seat with his feet up on the dash, like a boy. His talk drove a wedge into Henry's character, widening him. What Henry truly remembered, in a way that he was only beginning to understand, was the dark prairie of hair on Van's forearm, the surf at his collar: the places on men that he only now allows himself to see. Henry dances the salt and pepper shakers in his hands for an hour, angling up to his confession. It is difficult to be honest with the people you find beautiful.

"I feel about twenty years late to this, but I think I just finally found out I am…," Henry says, "someone who is…"

"Gay," Van says with a sly grin. "I'll have that beer now." Henry's surprised at his drinking, but Van shrugs. "Special occasions." They toast two chaste, low-carb bottles. Van claims he knew about Henry all along, telling him that it's theatre and "Everybody's gay-ish." This alights Henry's sense of an opening. Van, too, then…? On his departure, Van hugs him tightly and Henry registers that a man has never held him so forcefully, so intimately. The sheer surface area nearly makes him puddle.

"Congratulations Chief," Van says lightly into his ear. "You'll never have boring sex again." Van's hot breath makes new weather across Henry's interior life. He wants so badly to tell Van that they've been lovers for months, that it's about time he knows.

"You gonna be okay?" Van asks, at Henry's sudden tears.

Henry waves him off. "Allergies."

HENRY'S DAUGHTER COMES by with throw rugs, donuts, a scented candle the size of a layer cake which gives him headaches. She is in college in the city, and to his amazement, now that he is damaged, she's taken more of an interest in him, like the three-legged hamster she had as a child. When Henry speaks to Margot, by phone, once a week, she makes him feel as though his new life is a lunge from a moving vehicle. But Effie is Florence Nightingale to Henry's foot-soldier, off in a war where the opposing armies touch penises. They're good together; raising her was the one thing he did well. She even wants to help him write a personal ad, for Craigslist or Manhunt or DaddyCentral or the cavalcade of humiliations online, but some things your daughter cannot help you do.

"CuriousFather," he types. It sounds strange to him, his new name, if it is a name. He decides he is Oral Versatile, a box he'd never thought he'd have to check in this world. He crops Margot out of a photograph of the two of them and posts it.

Within an hour, he has responses. The first is from a teenager in Poughkeepsie who asks him if he has back-hair. The second, from FurCoach06, wants to know his feelings on "cock-fighting". He wades, blindly, through the acronyms, NSA, LTR, PNP, 4:20, P.A., T but V..., but the abbreviations do not end — the dynamic itself feels abrupt, hurried, capitalized. He chats with a lanky (and shirtless) young man named ThckReggie "in publishing" who comes on very strong, who asks him "U cam?" before he even knows Henry's name. "Wanna get off?" comes the next email. Followed by a link to pornographic website. Then comes the realization that Henry has been talking to a script, a robot of some sort, for the past fifteen minutes.

The next day, driving home and feeling frustrated and combustible, Henry makes eye contact with another driver. He looks a little like Van in eyebrows, but darker, more heavy-set, in a crisp white dress-shirt. At a full-stop, he winks at Henry and lifts himself to display his cock, masting out from the waistband of sweatpants. It's all Henry needs to choke on the possibility. For twenty minutes, Henry follows him to a giant, suburban house, somewhere in the wilds of Bridgewater. Margot would have loved the block, Henry thinks as he parks at the curb, this ideal degree of dappled light and tended hedges. Henry watches the other driver step out of his car — he's squatter, more thuggish than he thought. Then man unmistakably adjusts his erection and shakes his head at Henry, decisively, brutally, No, and vanishes inside.

Emboldened, Henry crosses the front lawn and pushes through rhododendrons and thorn-bush to peek in the bay window. On a long console table, track lights halo a bowl of polished stones. He can see the backside of a row of framed photos. Henry decides that he has come this far out of his way, he deserves something. He goes to the front door, knowing with every step that he is turning into a monster. In the glass pane, his reflection shocks him. His gray hair tufts out in all directions. Scratches on his face, like he's crawled all the way here, to this exact moment.

A woman opens the door. "Can I help you?" she asks. The other driver, Henry's prize, cowers on carpeted stairs. Henry can feel the secret becoming a knife.

"I'm sorry," Henry says. "I'm so completely lost."

THREE WEEKS LATER, Henry is on the train upstate to Dawn Manor. He's been instructed to get off at a small station where the Dawn Manor van will pick him up. "We'll be doing body work," Bodi Charles told him over the phone. "Make sure to bring comfortable clothing." Henry gazed down his front, his new middle. In the stress of the separation, Effie's donuts and the nachos for dinner, he no longer has comfortable clothing. Everything feels like a vice.

A nondescript minivan idles in the station lot. The driver jumps out and throws open the passenger door. He wears a leather jacket and black t-shirt with the word "Juicy" stitched in sequins. Henry is fairly certain Effie has the same one. This is "Spike," and his handshake, Henry is reassured to find, is vigorous with heterosexuality. His face and scalp are as smooth as glazed ceramic except for a brown goatee so elegantly manicured it could be topiary. Henry sits as far back in the van as possible, the only passenger.

"Don't you want to sit up front?" Spike asks.

"I like it in the rear," Henry says and Spike cocks an eyebrow. Immediately, Henry's convinced that he's made a gross miscalculation, that's he's too old, too unjuicy for saving. He hates it in the rear actually – he gets carsick.

The densely forested road gives way to acres of rolling hills. Henry feels out of joint in such a remote and rustic place; if he's going to find himself, it's going to be somewhere off the Garden State Parkway, near Indian food and cloverleaf intersections. Spike turns into a long gravel driveway, where a peace-flag bolted to a roadside maple only increases Henry's sense of personal doom.

"Look, I've changed my mind. Could you take me back to the train station?"

Spike answers, "There's only one train a day."

"I'll stay at a hotel."

"There's no hotel."

"Then I'll call a cab," Henry says.

But Spike has already parked in front of the Manor, a three-story Victorian painted, of all possible colors, purple. A wooden double-door, impeccably restored, opens on a broad porch with empty rocking chairs. The house is surrounded, on three sides, by forest.

"You've come this far Henry," Spike says. "Try going a little bit further."

Henry steps out of the van, closes his eyes. He takes a moment to notice the cold, a private sign that he is one year older. Soon, his December birthday will come and go and he may never answer the questions his body is asking.

"OK," Henry says. "Show me."

In the hardwood foyer, an over-long pussy-willow branch teeters in a vase like an accusatory finger. Above the telephone hangs a photographic portrait of the golden retriever slavering in a swatch of autumn light. Henry counts six arm-chairs in the living room and nothing else. The place seems willfully under-decorated, as if everything might need to be rearranged or cleared for yoga mats and trust falls. This is precisely how Margot always wanted their home to be — airy, uncluttered. Perhaps now it is, since he was the clutter.

"So no alcohol, no drugs, no sex, and no plastics," Spike says, leading Henry up the narrow stairs. "Bodi is environmentally sensitive."

"Plastics?" Henry asks.

"Some guys think they can bring their rubber gear anywhere."

On the second floor, wedged under one of the gables, is Henry's room. It's the sort of space people turn into a crypt of bad clothing and exercise equipment. A blond young man, Henry guesses mid-20s, lays on one of two twin beds like a deposited doll. He's dressed in a puffy, orange hunting jacket and loafers without socks. With a small terror, Henry understands that this is his roommate.

"You know, Jed," Spike says, "you can take off your jacket."

"Are there no single rooms?" Henry asks as kindly, diplomatically, as possible. Jed snorts.

"Everybody gets a roommate," Spike explains, one hand on the door-knob which, Henry notices, does not have a lock. "If we put people in singles, they just close off to the process."

"The process…?" Henry says.

"Of integrating… And actualizing…. Oh don't ask me," Spike says. "I just cook and fluff the pussy willow." Spike leaves them to get acquainted.

Henry sits on other bed and Jed hugs himself petulantly. Neither of these two people, it occurs to Henry, were in the goddamn brochure.

"So are you cold?" Henry asks. "Is it cold here?"

Jed eyes him bluntly, shaking his head. He has sharp, blue eyes. "So are you gay?"

"I have been married for twenty two years…," Henry begins but stops. He's not sure where the story goes after that.

Jed leans back. "Thank god."

B ODI'S EYES FIX Henry and every man in the living room. "It's the secrets that kill us," he says. "The cure for secrets is stories."

Dawn Manor's resident guru sits in the only leather armchair in the living room, wearing a linen shirt and flowy pants that are basically drapes. He's greyhound-thin, with rimless glasses and the flexibilities of a man half his age; every now and again, he lifts himself up on the arm-rests, like a gymnast on the bars, and tucks his feet underneath to sit cross-legged. Henry has noticed how Bodi touches things – tabletops, shoulders – with intense, appraising grace. Bodi was an antiques-dealer in "a prior life," he told them over the first breakfast. "It made me understand that everything has a delicacy that must be protected."

Four men face Bodi in a scattershot arrangement. Across from Henry, Jed sits on his hands and contemplates his kneecaps. Of the group, Henry is by far the oldest.

"How about you, Doug?" Bodi says, hands resting upwards on his knees. "Tell us the story of your secret."

Doug's baleful gaze relocates from the window to Bodi. In a cowboy shirt and stained jeans, Doug spooks Henry. He gives off stray voltage, mumbling his reluctance under his breath. Even his moustache doesn't look completely enlisted. Doug works a cigarette from his pocket and Bodi stops him.

"I just want to roll it between my fingers," Doug says. "Helps me relax."

Doug worked in a shipyard in Bayonne, he explains, running the cranes, and "pruning up" in the showers. "I was Jiffy Lube. In and out," Doug says, and Henry shivers with a revulsion that almost instantly becomes intrigue. Doug's boss showed up, fucked him, and fired him the next day. "Those were union showers," Doug says. "Asshole was management."

He lights the cigarette and Bodi says with impressive calm, a first show of authority, "Put the cigarette out or go outside." Doug smirks and lopes out to the porch.

Bodi threshes his hands, recovering the moment. "Henry, what about you? Would you like to say something?"

Henry looks for an entrance, a beginning to what seems like hopeless years of middle. He sees the ghostly white bridge of Scott Malcolm's forearm reaching into his sleeping bag at Boy Scout Camp circa 1963. He remembers, as a teenager, imagining his parents dying in a plane crash so he could live with the tenor Jussi Bjorling in his Italian castle and hold Bjorling's penis in his hand whenever he wanted to, the secret root of his talent. Then, with a stab of self-loathing, Henry recalls the certain fold and tuck to the coverlet on the guest bed. "In the early part of my marriage," Henry starts, and it's like working a pale, dense nut free from inside him, "I started this extension to my house that I never finished…"

At the edge of the driveway, Henry and three others stand in a confused huddle, trying to fix a snow-break. At noon, Bodi sent the men out to the lawn to work. "Across cultures, across time, men go outside to go inside," he told them. A day in, and the platitude per minute of speech ratio is getting to Henry. It's as if Bodi has learned to turn every sentence inside out, like a sock. Henry holds a notched wooded brace while Doug sets two 4 X 4s into it. Another man, short and talkative, hammers at the juncture point, missing as much as not. His nametag reads "Ronnie!" He works as an inspector for the Transit Authority, which means, he told Henry with relish, he can cruise every truck-stop on the Turnpike while getting paid.

"This was supposed to be some singles thing," Doug announces, blowing air into his fist. "Except it turns out I paid eight hundred bucks to come here and fix this guy's lawn. Fucking joke."

Jed, standing uselessly nearby in his jacket and loafers, giggles.

Doug shoots back, "You think eight hundred bucks is ha ha?" Jed retracts his hands inside the sleeves of his jacket, holes up.

Since the morning, Henry has been feeling increasingly remote, like he has tickets to his life except they're last row, obscured view. What did he come for? None of the men seem like prospects to him; they're all as warped and lonely as he is. With a pang, he realizes he's missing Van, back home, tending to his plants and mail. He must call.

Suddenly, a brown-black flutter of wings explodes from behind the trees. Canadian geese, assembling into a V.

Jed asks, "How far do they go?"

"Delaware, Maryland…," Henry says.

"Outside Bethesda, some guy held a knife to my throat until I swallowed," Ronnie says. "That's Maryland in a nutshell."

Gunshots pop from behind the Manor, out of view. Henry flinches – he's heard shots before, in the city, but he always told himself that it was a car backfiring, fireworks. But these shots are close and unmistakable. Hunters. The geese go wild, squawking.

Henry notices that there are tears rolling down Jed's cheeks, and the kid makes no effort to wipe them away. "It's something that happens sometimes, from my meds," Jed says. "I don't have control over it." Ronnie hums the Twilight Zone theme but Henry makes him quit.

With relief, Henry hears the peel of a bell at the front porch: Bodi calling them inside. Doug collects the tools and shoves them at Jed, saying, "Since you didn't do jack shit today." As the others head back, but Henry lingers with Jed. They're roommates, after all, and this is what roommates do. He notices, at his ankle, a little strip of bluing skin. Even in the cold, the kid's not wearing any socks. Up close, out here in the bracing cold, he sees that Jed is older than he thought, with difficult skin. He's not so much young as preserved. Jed's father runs a Christian school somewhere, and last night, Jed took out a portable Bible to read from the "gay part". "Goliath was 'uncircumcised,'" Jed whispered. Henry said, turning off the light, "Look, don't give me nightmares."

Out in the dusk, Henry puts his hand on Jed's shoulder, the gesture he can think of. With an expectant look, Jed follows Henry's hand to his face, registering a proposition.

"Am I what you're looking for?" Jed asks.

Henry says and removes his hand. "I'm not looking."

Jed's face goes flat. "You're too old and fat anyway."

Henry leaves him burdened with the tools, thinking: Go ahead and freeze.

LUNCH IS SPIKE in a Mexican peasant shirt and shorts, delivering their plates to the table and flexing his biceps. He could be working the Leisure Deck of a cruise.

"Should we save some food for Rigby?" Ronnie asks.

Bodi takes a quick breath and straightens. Spike pulls up close to him. Rigby had a stroke two weeks ago, he says, and for the first time, seeing them together, Henry realizes this is partly what Dawn

Manor sells, the miracle they're all there for: two grown men, leaning into each other.

"It was horrible and spasmy," says Spike, "and like froth was coming out of her mouth—"

Bodi interrupts him. "—Please Spike…"

Spike and Bodi excuse themselves and retire behind a door marked "Private", their area the house. A lock slides home.

"Guys," Ronnie says, "Who do you think is cuter, Bodi or Spike?"

Doug crashes his fork. "We just heard about a fucking dog dying."

The yearning here, Henry thinks, none of them is exempt. Henry decides he has to leave, before he turns into one of these people. He locates the phone, underneath the framed Rigby portrait. His gaze coalesces on the well-chewed Barbie in her mouth. A brass caption reads, "Rigby, Gender Warrior." Henry dials Van's cell.

"I want out of here," Henry tells him.

"Is it a cult?" Van says. "Tell me and I'll get the Better Business Bureau to do an airlift."

He hears, faintly, the clink of ice in a glass. Henry stays silent, making room for Van's dynamic to take over. And he does, telling him that his ex-wife is moving to Orlando, and that she's taking his son with her. "Now I realize why people kidnap their children," Van says. "What's the jail time on that?"

"Are you drinking?" Henry asks, and from the quiet he knows that he's right. But he's in no position to challenge anyone on their contradictions. If anything, he feels honored that Van raided the liquor cabinet, that he had something Van needed.

"We have to look out for each other," Henry says.

"Roger that, Chief."

"You're my closest friend," Henry says, wincing at the truth of it.

"I know," Van says, "and I just really feel bad about that."

THROUGH THE LIVING room windows, Henry watches snow streak down, blanketing the lawn, and feels a creeping dread. A blizzard is beginning and for two more days, he's going to be stuck here, with these people trying to pry him open. Bodi hands out dozens of red strips of ribbon. They're supposed to tie one to each part of their bodies that has experienced a "wounding." "I did this at a men's conference in Sedona," Bodi says, "and by the end, there was just this sea of red."

Doug throws his ribbons to the floor. "Bullshit."

"Nobody said this would be easy," Bodi says.

"Nobody said this caca works," Doug answers. "I'm going out."

But with the front door wide, Doug stops short at the threshold. "Holy fuck," Doug says. "You might want to look at this."

Emblazoned across the door, in crude red spray paint, is the word FAGGOTS. It takes Henry some time to understand that the graffiti refers to him. He has never been called a faggot before, and now, in shock, he realizes he is hated for the love that he's yet to experience. Bodi calls the police and there's some brief, terse negotiation about an incident report. "Don't you pay taxes up here?" Ronnie says to Bodi while he's on the phone. "There should be fences! And guns!"

Bodi wants everyone in for the night, but Doug has vanished outside. Henry offers to fetch him. During moments of stress, Henry wants assignments, distracting lists. It's the stage manager in him. Before he's out the door, Ronnie hands him a can of mace and whispers, "Remember Bethesda."

Out on the lawn, the snow slants horizontally. Henry spies Doug a ways up the drive, hammering at the snow-break. Henry approaches with his hands in his pockets, like a sullen teen, but he feels a passing moment of luck, as though he stepped out from underneath a bullseye. FAGGOTS, Henry thinks. Some neighbor kid learning to use fear. He wonders how Bodi will rescue the weekend. At least, Henry thrills to think, they'll skip the body work.

A bright orange flash moves at his periphery and Henry takes an instinctive step back. At the edge of the forest, a hunter emerges from the trees, dressed in camouflage pants and cap. He carries a goose over his shoulder, its neck twisted like a gunny sack. In his left hand, a double-barrel shotgun points into the ground. The hunter nods to Henry and unzips his fly. An arc of piss steams the air.

"You didn't see who did that to the front of the house, did you?" Henry calls out.

The hunter looks back at the door, not bothering to conceal himself on the turn. "Somebody did a little job, eh?" he says with a smirk in his yellowing beard. "You one of the gays?"

"I guess so," Henry answers. The hunter laughs, shakes off, and tucks himself back into his pants.

"I hope you get to figuring that one out," he says. Then he adds with a warming drawl, "I'll tell you this. You know that dog they had running around here? Getting into people's business?"

"I just got here."

"Well, you tell Mr. Charles I know who poisoned her."

Henry only wanted to slip in and out of this place a better, less confused person. He never wanted to be a messenger, an actor in anything. Except now he has this news, that Bodi and Spike's neighbors are more cruel than they know. The weekend pivots into greater darkness. When the hunter tips his head and heads back into the forest, Henry rushes back to the Manor, determined to throw this information off him, rid his mind of it. The dog, the graffiti, they aren't his problems. When he reenters the living room, Bodi has made a fire.

"I need to talk to you," Henry says.

Bodi makes him tell the story twice. Ronnie gasps at every detail until Bodi shoots him a chilling look. "She wasn't your dog. Stop over-reacting."

Ronnie's clearly wounded. "Over-reacting is what I'm good at."

A hard rap hits the front door, and the men go silent. Henry's pulse skips, imagining a mob outside with torches, pitchforks, hoes – rusty, upstate kind of weapons.

"Is this Dawn Manor?" a voice asks.

"Don't open the door!" Ronnie yells and moves behind one of the armchairs. "It's a trap! I've seen this movie!"

The voice is familiar to Henry, but the shock of it strikes him dumb. Bodi unlatches the door and the radiator in Henry's chest takes a kick, fires on. Van walks into the parlor in his corduroy jacket, hiking boots, a long knitted cap folded in his hands like a gift.

Van asks, "Did I miss the fun part?"

SPIKE RECOGNIZES THE hunter by the detail of the beard, a man named Bailey, and calls him with cool efficiency, revving into anger. It seems a neighbor, a widow, paid two high-school kids to feed Rigby a steak laced with ketamine. Retribution, Henry learns, for some damage the dog caused to a pheasant farm. "I've done ketamine," Spike tells Bodi. "And I can tell you it is so deeply fucked up that I can't even tell you."

Henry stands impatiently with them, corralled as the witness, while Van mixes with the crowd in the living room. The fact that his friend, his possession, is socializing bothers him immeasurably. "Can I go?" he asks and it triggers Spike's sense of action — they will confront the widow tonight. When Bodi tells him the idea is ridiculous, Spike answers him with a single, sharp laugh, and Henry glimpses into their private dynamic, the corners of dismissal and condescension. As he edges away, leaving them to argue, the last thing he hears is Spike saying, with vivifying power, "If we bring the police into this, we look like cowards, and this gay man is not a coward," and Bodi answering, "Would you stop saying 'This gay man' please?"

In the parlor, Van sits on the floor, rubbing his eyes. The sleeves on his shirt are rolled back and, in the firelight, his forearms look lathed. Henry feels a surge of ownership. Van pats the back of Henry's calf, a contact that blooms long after Van removes his hand.

"So are you Henry's boyfriend?" Ronnie asks.

"I'm more of an evacuation team," Van answers. A flask nestles between his legs.

"Drinking's not allowed," Henry says. "You should hide it."

"Yeah well," Doug says, nabbing the flask, "this whole weekend is off the handle." He throws back two shots and dashes it under his thigh when Bodi approaches.

With a tight, dark expression — a coerced look Henry recognizes from his own marriage — Bodi explains that they're going out. Ronnie tells him that they're crazy to leave, but Spike will not be delayed. They gather their jackets and are gone. Left to themselves, the men look at each other tentatively.

"Can we talk for a minute?" Henry says to Van. "In my room."

Jed corrects him, "Our room."

Van slinks behind him, which makes Henry feel like a scold. Once in the garret, Van stretches on the bed, his eyes red and raw. "You wouldn't believe the roads coming up here," he says. "Like that production of A Christmas Carol where the snow-rigging broke. God, Mrs. Cratchit had great tits."

"Are you high?" Henry asks. "Drunk and high?"

"I know, I'm a disaster. Trust me, you're not the only one who thinks that."

Henry sits across from Van. Van is living in the same pair of corduroys, same plaid shirt he last saw him in. He's cagey and restless, a stray animal.

"Why did you come?" Henry asks, hoping for one kind of answer.

"I was going out of my mind," Van says. "You gave me a mission."

Van rises and casually sifts through the closet. Out comes a stack of handkerchiefs, all different colors. Van shakes them out. "Is there some kind of homosexual karate belt system that I'm not aware of?"

"Those are not mine," Henry says, finding relief in a subject that is not either of them. "They're my roommate's. Jed. The drugged-up little monster. I'm sure you saw him."

Van pulls a brown pill bottle from the closet and examines the label. "Haldol," he says with a whistle. "This is the primo shit."

Jed lets himself in, without a knock. Van tries to shove the pills back onto the closet shelf before he can notice, but Jed catches him. "What are you doing? You're going through my things."

Van cooks up a lie, the search for a blanket, and Henry likes seeing Van's awkwardness. It levels them somehow.

"So…do you ever take that jacket off?" Van asks Jed.

"You don't really care," Jed says. "Nobody cares."

"Come on, Jed, you're wrong," Henry says. The lie strains him.

"You just called me a 'drugged-up monster,'" Jed says with a total absence of affect. "I heard you."

Henry apologizes, feeling hateful. He and Jed, the oldest and the youngest, they are the two last boys to be picked, and they need to band together. "We're all trying here," Henry says, but trying for what? To be themselves, finally, and it is exhausting.

Jed announces that he's going to take a walk. It's plainly a bad idea, but Henry wants his time with Van, and he won't stop him. Once Jed is gone — they listen for his footsteps on the stairs — Henry whispers, "You see what this place is like."

Van lies down on the bed, against Henry, oblivious to his power. "Maybe it's good for you," he says. "We both know you need to get over me." And the shock of its delivery detonates Henry's hope. All these months, Van knew his secret desire and now reads it aloud like a boring headline.

Henry wills himself to sit up and grab for what he loves. Instead, he rests his hand on Van's knee, the closest he can come. "Let me take care of you," Henry says, risking everything.

"Don't," Van says.

"What?"

Van pats Henry's hand. "That, what your hand is doing. I'm on the wrong team."

Henry feels the moment between them dilating, narrowing to a point. "I don't think you're on anybody's team."

Van lifts his hand off his thigh and deposits it on the mattress. "And now I will avail myself of a libation," he says, a borrowed line from a play, surely, some ironic brush-off. Van heads out and Henry hammers his pillow. The question that he came up here to answer — who can I love? — is not a question after all. It is an impossibility. The downstairs phone rings and continues to ring. Henry yells for someone to answer it. Finally, when the ringing stops, Henry notices a new silence.

Downstairs, the men are missing and the door into Spike and Bodi's private area is wide open. From within, he hears the murmur of voices and smells a heavy muddle of incense. Henry finds the private den where Van and the others have collected, sipping coffee cups with liquor. In a recliner in the center of the room, Van smokes a joint and looks faintly territorial.

"Guys, I want to tell you, before this clusterfuck ends," Doug says from the couch, already clumsily drunk. "I just want to say that Doug isn't my real name. It's Leslie."

Ronnie nods, fiddling with the stereo. "Now it all makes sense."

"Welcome Chief," Van says coolly and improbably offers him a toke. Henry grits his teeth and wills a sense of accountability at him.

"This is a really bad idea," Henry says.

As a stage manager, Henry is known for his quiet control, a firm hand at the end of Equity breaks, but now he sees the fantasy of it. He has no intrinsic authority, only what is given to him. So he sits on a coach and surrenders. When Doug passes along the joint, Henry takes a single, ferocious toke, welcoming the chance for a new personality.

"So Van, if you're not Henry's boyfriend," Ronnie asks. "Are you anybody's boyfriend?"

Van grins and there's this one crazy tooth that can still break Henry's loyal heart. "Nah," Van says with an odd restraint. It's as if he wants to pass here, among them. Ronnie swings around to Van's side and begins giving Van a shoulder massage with a boldness Henry can only imagine. "You know you have great hair," Ronnie says. "It's muy Pirates of Penzance." Van closes his eyes and the recliner goes back that much further.

"Why don't you tell us a little about you?" Ronnie says.

With drunken volition, Van begins a rambling story about his ten year-old son. When he had bad leg cramps, Van would massage them every night, before bed. "His little kid-muscles were amazing," Van finishes, marveling at a remote, private happiness. "Nothing in the world had taught him to be scared." Then Van turns his head to the side and, it pains Henry to see, cries.

"What'd I do?" Ronnie mouths.

"Leave him alone," Henry says. But as Ronnie starts to retract his hand, Van grabs it, keeps it on him. Van swipes his face and replies, "It's fine. Keep going."

He watches as Ronnie's hands undo the top buttons of Van's shirt, combing into the hair at the base of his neck. "It's all right that I do this?" Ronnie asks, intuiting some deeper need. "Take it easy," Van says, but he's not really fighting as Ronnie moves further down his front. Van groans once, a sound in their years of friendship Henry has never heard him make. The room suddenly seems more dense, a hot close dream. A tiny metallic clack: Doug undoing his belt. "That's right," Doug says, his eyes jumping all over Van's body, like he's checking to see how pieces of machinery come together. He releases his own penis from his jeans, a peachy thumb, and kneels between Van's legs. The teeth of a zipper open.

"What are you doing?" Henry says quietly, catching a glimpse of a white blade of flesh at Van's groin before he closes his eyes. He hears the rustle and give of the leather recliner, the rake of Ronnie's fingers. Doug's smacking noises become fiendish wet. It would be so easy for Henry to join, to take his piece of the moment. He's close enough to feel the transgression with his hands. "Fuck yeah," Doug say over and over, in a hungry loop.

Henry walks, calmly, decisively, out of the room. He can't watch Van be taken, fed upon. There are certain rules to things. Aren't there rules? He takes the stairs two a time, back to his room where he sits on the bed, blood thumping and disoriented. He throws open the window and gulps in the cold. Across the lawn, Jed, in his orange coat, trudges in the snow at the perimeter of the house lights. Henry calls out to him, the other exile, but Henry discovers he has nothing to say. So he waves hello. Jed waves back, sweetly, like they're two boys departing from each other after an evening of play. Then he moves further and further out until Henry can no longer see him at all.

Henry awakes in his clothes. He stares at the bed across the room until he realizes that it is immaculate, the way Jed had left it the night before. He never came back from his walk. The night reconstitutes itself, finally, as emergency.

He heads downstairs to alert Bodi and finds Van on the living room floor, cocooned in a crocheted blanket. His shoes and socks are off and Henry sees on Van's right foot a little meadow of hair split by a scar, a scar about which Henry will never know the story. Henry nudges him.

"What?" Van asks, bleary.

He takes a moment to memorize Van's face, slack from sleep, the closest he'll ever come. With relief, Henry feels nothing, the end of an idea. It's not a kiss Henry wants, but a chance to be known, fully, in this life. Finally, he knows where not to look.

"You need to leave, now," he says.

Bodi exits from his private room and gives Henry a non-committal nod. The men must have cleaned up, erased the night from the room. They will get away with it. Bodi goes to the front window to stare at the two feet of snow piled against the door, the heap of the night's weather. When Henry tells him about Jed's absence, Bodi's face collapses. "Oh Christ, my fucking insurance."

He rings the house bell and Doug and Ronnie slowly assemble in the foyer, purposefully missing each other's eyes. Bodi asks them to go looking, and Henry's outside first, happy to be free of the house. He punches through the deep carpet of snow, going to the trees. At the forest threshold, he turns back to look at the men, splintering across the lawn, each alone and searching.

About fifty yards into the woods, Henry comes across Jed, propped against a spruce. At some point in the night, Jed unbuttoned his orange jacket, and Henry sees there is nothing underneath. No shirt, just his skin covered by a ramp of snow climbing up to his neck. His face is glazed, but his eyes find Henry when he kneels beside him. Inside the lining of Jed's jacket, tucked in the pocket, is a can with a red cap. Spray paint.

"Leave me here," Jed says, barely over a whisper. "I'm not right."

Henry takes the paint can and palms it. The metal is frigid to the touch, nearly empty, and the ball inside clacks ably. Henry tosses the can into the woods, as far as he can. It's a good throw, a good release. "You're coming with me," Henry says, committing to it. Then he curls his arms around the boy and lifts.

JOAN LARKIN

Studies for a Crucifixion
after Francis Bacon

Oil smeared with dust
to last: lush rage-orange.

Meat splayed on a table.
The business-suited, rubber-

suited stare elsewhere.
Black windows gape.

Meat hangs from lucite,
thick green line touching.

Centered: meat odalisque
on smeared bed. Meat-nothing––

BRENT CALDERWOOD

Headless Men

"We had faces then. You could tell a story with your eyes and face."
—Norma Desmond, *Sunset Boulevard*

"We had faces then."
A line from a movie no one sees.
They are all headless men.

We used to read books in a leather den,
then head to the tearoom on our knees.
We had faces then.

Now we're online till god-knows-when
for a knight with a horse in his BVDs,
but they are all headless men,

either chopped at the neck like a free-range hen
or cropped at the crotch like limbless trees.
We had faces; then

we found gyms—and amen!—
we could be beautiful, built to please.
Perfect, headless men.

I wish we'd take to the streets again
and fight for love or against disease.
We had faces then.
Now we're headless men.

Dolly Parton, I Just Want Everything to Feel Good

I got rhythm and he got whiskey   we drink Jameson for Rusty Nails
We get drunk. We go down into the subbasement,   stand up fuck. The lights go out
after I've come to dirt and Fedler into his wife   beater. Me and Fedler then up
in the woods, naked. Ohio River   crawling out, smiles scratched on us.
I'd follow you into dark anywhere   if the lumber jack stanced there,
sipping cigarette milk. You are lucky,   I am me. I believe there is nothing wrong
with tug and pull, as long as you don't want   everything. Some men are messy stretching
stomachs, gulping your body all night   inside the Blue Anchor. You would like it there
Loretta Lynn on the jukebox   I play her over and over until she gets stupid enough
to agree with me people change little   if at all.

Dolly Parton, What About a Bed the Size of Texas?

He knew not to Greyhound urinal, so it reasons   when a man says seeing his tattoos
disappear into someone's ass is spiritual,   Zsa-Zsa would dash his cigarette,
thanking the evening, but no. Wait to laugh, Dolly   This is a reason you shouldn't
hole up. This Ohio desert   needs you. It never looks finished
It is a garage off the side of Zsa-zsa's house   I can still smell Oldsmobile
as I throw him across the room. He is unsure at first   When I leave, he hands me
Loretta Lynn, calls me sugar pants   I spend the night. In the front porch swing,
it is your early song. A whole movie   could be made of the walk to bed. We fuck
Generosity is something I like in a drink.   That's what Fedler said. It's sad
he didn't love me   in winter. I am much more beautiful

Ten Questions You Were Afraid to Ask, Answered

I.

The first time? I thought myself an infant, rooting the breast for
dinner. You too may feel
the seamless press of your body to a mirror,

the smudge of your own skin a ridiculousness that need Windex,
and quick. Embarrassed, I asked to be taken home,

but in the car was the bright green of her dashboard lights burning
the clean color of *go*.

2.

Years before. I even admitted it once to a woman that later sent me
poems about hummingbirds

dipping their beaks into feeders full of cocaine dissolved in sweet,
red water.

3.

Finally came summer, my summer of plain clothing—unironed
and cotton and bland— nothing afraid

to get dirty, nothing afraid to be slicked with mud, the forest
coming off in a happy heap
on the tent floor.

It was the summer I allowed myself to be bitten enough that the
welps rose but dissolved back by bedtime; it was the summer I
finally said

come, mother mosquitoes, my reddest blood is ready for your young.

4.
Stupid things, mostly. That's how I wasted most of my worry—
dumb-ass questions that do not matter. Who should open

the door? Who to pay for dinner? Who to lean in first with whose
hands braced strong to the jawline? Who in the tie, who in the
dress, and what about all this long, long hair?

5.
 Consider this: a woman's pH is between that of wine and bread.
An imperfect leaven, the kind of crust that betrays the softness

inside. Cooled to the heat of your mouth, its sweetness dipped in a
dry red, the aftertaste of that one oyster you had

from the other coast. You were slightly repulsed, but then the
fisherman pulled it straight from his bucket for you, cut it free

with a small, curved knife.

6.
You will miss it. Not the man but the normal
the man brings.

7.
Unfortunately. All the time. In the grocery, a mother swung her
arm to corral her daughter
behind her, protecting her from us—the contagions behind.

We were hurt, but we stayed in line; we waited our turn. We smiled
at the child peeking from behind the thick coat, and because it was
a good day, we felt a little sorry for the mother. In our basket was
red tomatoes and yellow peppers, a riot of greens, the unbelievable
brightness of

all we had chosen.

8.
The strawberry is a fruit unshamed of its seeds. Make no mistake
how it is textured
as the tongue.

9.
Thirty years old.

10.
Too late? Perhaps, but only when you think of evening, the song full
and crickets volleying the trees,

the sound from one side then the other, a saturation that can carry
the young
down the black river of who they think they should be.

Think instead of morning. Not the thin monotony of weak light,
but that low, constant pleasuring of the air

that doesn't try so hard but simply tips your ears
with light.

YINKA ROSE REED-NOLAN

They Call Us Crazy

'M SIXTEEN AND MY hair is bushy and wild. It hasn't been flat ironed in almost a month, so I've been forced to alternate between letting it flow wildly and winding it into tight Zulu knots. Today felt like a wild day or maybe I was too lazy to part and twist my hair this morning. Leah offered to braid my hair last week, but I don't like Leah. I can't decide if I don't like her because everyone else loves her or if it's because she is overdrawn and exaggerated like her name. L-E-A-H. Four letters is one too many. Her name should be spelled L-I-A like the girl who sleeps in the bed next to mine. They are on name alert, Leah and Lia, but it's easy to tell them apart, overstated and not.

My feelings about Leah have nothing to do with the way she spells her name; it's the way she acts. She manufactures lies like Santa's elves manufacture Christmas toys. And the worst part is I can see her cranking the wheel in her mind to indent lies in the air so clearly that she hands them out like receipts people can fold and carry in their pockets. Leah is a slippery fifteen year old who talked her way into getting us a cabinet full of candy. The cabinet is locked of course, but once a day we can have our pick of candy. Sounds great, right, but the four of us who have the candy cabinet are eating disordered. We don't want candy, or, at least I know I don't and I'm pretty sure

Leah doesn't either. Craving candy was another lie aimed at chiseling some time off of her sentence behind the locked double doors of Herring Psychiatric Hospital. It's hard to escape anyone on the girls unit where we live, but it's especially hard to escape Leah.

The regular girls who are depressed, suicidal, bipolar or schizophrenic eat at two long rectangular tables between the kitchen counter and the lounge area where we have groups. The four of us eating disordered girls sit at a tiny square table by the window. We are our own island with our own staff monitor and our own rules. No talking about body image or weight at meals. No talking about food, whether you like the food on your tray or not. And you have to eat everything on your tray or you have to have a Resource (or maybe two depending on how much food you leave behind). When I first got here, two weeks ago, I didn't know what a Resource was, and it didn't sound so bad. When Jude, the patron staff of our lost eating disordered souls, told me I could either eat the rest of my disgusting veggie burger that tasted like grilled rice and soiled mustard or complete two Resources (using the word complete was a trick), I eagerly chose the two Resources.

Hearty bulimic Hannah, who eats tums three times a day for calcium and heartburn, shook her head in warning, but Jude shot her a sharp look. I didn't understand what could be so bad about a Resource or two. I thought Jude would drop an encyclopedia type book in front of me and I'd have to write something about coping skills. Instead Jude got up and headed to the refrigerator that is only unlocked during meals. "Chocolate or vanilla?" She asked.

"What?" I replied confused.

Jude held up a boxed nutrition drink much like Ensure and repeated, "Chocolate or vanilla?"

"Uh, one of each?"

She returned to the table with two drinks and smiled, "You've got fifteen minutes."

I nearly gagged as the taste of musky vanilla syrup flooded my mouth.

"I told you that you didn't want a Resource," Hannah said, knowing that she is always right.

"Hannah you know the rules," Jude warned, "do I need to get you a Resource?"

Hannah quietly went back to shoveling the mac and cheese off her tray and I finished gulping down my first drink. Jude slid me the other one with a satisfied grin on her face. She may be the food police, but it's hard to hate Jude with her sly smile and strawberry blonde hair that smells like cinnamon. Even if everyone says, "leave it to Jude to ruin your day," I kind of like her because when she works nights she always lets me stay up past lights out so we can talk about my day. Leah, on the other hand, has no redeeming qualities.

An hour before staff change, we have our snack. A tray of cookies and juice cups are set out in the kitchen for the regular girls, while I sit in front of the nurses' station with Hannah, Leah and Ashley, a girl who has been known to jump up in the middle of a meal and declare that nothing tastes as good as thin feels. Jude oversees as we open white paper bags that contain our special order snacks. I find that I get off easy today; I only have a cranberry juice cup and a box of raisin granola, while Leah, who likes to sit next to me, has a thick slice of cherry pie.

Once Jude has checked to make sure that our bags have all the food we're supposed to eat, we are allowed to begin the process of glorified indulgence. I tear my cereal box open to get to the pocket-sized bag of granola, then pinch the bag on either side and begin to pull. The bag isn't cooperating today, and I wish that a non-cooperating snack meant I didn't have to eat, but it doesn't, so I yank the bag with force and it rips open, exploding granola. Leah laughs loudly, causing Jude to look up from her cheese sandwich and frown at me and the granola in my hair.

"Sorry," I whisper to Jude.

"Clean it up," she says flatly and I think I may actually get out of snack until she gets up from her seat, warns us not to try anything funny and walks around the corner into the kitchen area. Jude is all knowing. She knows to quickly grab Ashley's tray when she is about to toss it off of the table, she knows that Hannah likes to sweet talk med nurse Patti into giving her milk of magnesia as a laxative and she even knows that I hide food in my socks. Unfortunately she doesn't know about Leah's lies, but even Leah knows that she isn't immune to an after meal strip search from Jude. There is no way we are going to try anything funny.

"I couldn't find any granola, so this will have to do," Jude says placing a box of cheerios in front of me.

I am more careful this time. I tear the box open, then slowly pull the bag open and begin to eat. I'm supposed to use a spoon and a bowl, but Jude is eating her sandwich and maybe feeling a little nice, so she lets me pour the cereal directly into my mouth. After a few crunches and a swallow, I break the rules and announce, "This tastes like nothing."

Jude looks up with a smile and tosses me a box of raisin bran, "Cheerios are nothing, which is why you are eating this box of cereal too."

I slouch down in my chair with only a pout because there is no arguing with Jude unless I want a third box of cereal. Leah bursts out laughing again and a wad of cherry pie flies out of her mouth and onto the table in front of her.

"It's really not that funny," I mutter.

"Sure it is," Leah assures me as she takes her hand, wipes it across the table and licks the pie from her fingers.

"At least I don't have fattening pie," I whisper quietly so Jude doesn't hear.

Leah turns to me and opens her mouth so I can see the cherry filling on her tongue, "The pie isn't so bad. It's a lot like when a boy shoots sperm in your mouth."

Slightly disgusted, I look at her blankly as she shovels another fork full of pie into her mouth and licks her lips before she continues with a loud moan, "Sperm is gooey and bitter, but it feels so good when a boy gives it to you in your mouth as a present."

"I wouldn't know," I say appalled and turn away from Leah.

Leah clicks her tongue and gasps dramatically, "We have to get you a boy then." She touches my bush of hair and smiles. I can tell she has got her wheels turning again. "You really should reconsider letting me do your hair. I can braid it in corn-rows like mine and then we can surely get one of the boys from the other unit to shoot sperm for you. "

I flinch in disgust and Jude is standing over us. She slaps a cookie down on the table in front of Leah and announces, "For inappropriate snack time conversation."

Hannah looks our way and shakes her head to say that she knew Leah was going to get extra food for that one and I shouldn't have sat next to her in the first place. Simply relieved that I didn't get a third box of cereal, I start on the box of raisin bran as Leah begins to fondle the cookie in front of her.

After snack, Lia, the one I like, is waiting for me. Humming a song, her body is perched on the window ledge by my bed with her legs dangling above the ground. She smiles sweetly as I enter the room and asks, "How was snack?"

"Psh, you know Jude," I reply as I flop down on my bed.

Lia smiles and nods, but she doesn't actually know Jude. At least not the way I do.

At the beginning of every shift staff gets to pick who they want to work with for the day and Jude always picks me and Hannah. I know this because Sheryl, who only gets to work with me on Sundays (Jude's day off), told me she was disappointed that Jude always snatches me up. I picture staff having fist fights every morning over who gets who and who is stuck with leftovers. It's nice to know that people want to have me and I'm not yesterday's dinner tray. I like Jude because she always picks me. It means she loves me and I love her too. I like Sheryl, and all, but I want to be just like Jude when I grow up. Maybe I don't want to be as mean, but I want to wear smart plaid pants, eat cheese sandwiches, and ask people questions when their mouths are full and then apologize for it because I used to be a waitress. Jude is smart, chic and tactfully passive aggressive. Sheryl is butch, dykish and direct; that just isn't me.

Lia usually gets chosen by Sarah and she seems happy about it. I wouldn't be unhappy if Sarah was my staff. Sarah's a little older than the other counselors, but Sarah manages to look cooler than them. She dyes her curly hair a color that is somewhere between violet and burgundy, has nose and lip rings and tattoos all over her body. My favorite is the one behind her ear that says "joy." Smiling, she explained that it was so joy could always whisper in her ear. I'm going to steal that tattoo from her, but mine is going to say "hope."

Kicking my feet against the mattress, I whine that "I have to pee."

"The bathroom is unlocked," Lia says quietly.

Because I am on eating disorder protocol, the only time we have free access to the bathroom is in the mornings before breakfast. Any other time of day and we have to ask for staff to unlock it, but Lia has never complained about the limitation. I jump up off the bed and scramble to find that she is right and the bathroom is unlocked.

"Score," I yell.

"You're only going to pee right?" Lia calls as she follows to the bathroom.

"Of course," I flash a smile.

"I'm going to watch," Lia announces knowing that every time I go to the bathroom, staff has to stand outside a cracked door and make sure I'm not purging.

"Do you also want to look in the toilet after I go?" Staff does this too.

"Not really," she laughs. "So, you have to sing."

"Sing?" I say as I push the door closed a little, and then pull down my pants.

"Yes, sing, so I know you're not throwing up."

"I don't know what to sing."

Without much thought, Lia suddenly begins harmonizing her favorite song. I don't know the song or the words, but I hum along loud enough to please her.

After I flush and wash my hands, I come out of the bathroom and I am met with a big Lia hug. "What's that for?" I ask as I return her embrace.

"Cause, you're awesome."

"Thanks," I walk to my bed and lay down. Lia follows, crawling into my bed and cuddling up next to me, "I wish I could feel your pain."

"That's sweet. I wouldn't want you to feel my pain though. I wish you didn't even have to feel you own," I turn my head and look at her. Her soft blond vegetation is spread across my pillow and she's gazing at me with the big upside down smiles that are her green eyes. Lia is a giant sunflower in a late summer corn field; even if she is depressive, she has a soft happiness.

She sits up and leans over me, "Let me feel your pain tonight, so I don't have to feel my own."

Her pain is written in the soft pink curves of scared skin. Lia has mapped out the abuse and betrayal for strangers to follow. Every scar represents something, she explained. She said they were like stars in the dark sky of her existence; they help her see the way. Lia thinks of herself as dark and twisted, but she is not manipulative or conniving like the other Leah, so I know she is light.

"What do you mean?" I ask.

Lia leans in slowly and her lips press against mine. Mouth sucking is gross, but this kiss from Lia is sweet. I hold back a smile and blush knowing what she means by "feel your pain." Lia pulls back, her eyes smiling in anticipation. I giggle and nod bashfully; I've never done anything before, but I will let Lia take my pain tonight. Her body floats back down next to mine and she drifts into a dreamy sleep that I follow.

W AKEY WAKEY, IT'S time to get up for dinner," a thick Russian accent infiltrates my dream and I feel a hand on my shoulder. I open my eyes to see Lubov standing over me. She must be my staff tonight. When I brace myself to get up, I hit the warmth of Lia sleeping next to me; it wasn't all a dream. My eyes look to Lubov nervously, but she is only waiting for me to get up. In Lubov's Russia it must not be unusual for two girls to sleep together in a twin sized bed, or maybe she doesn't care to get us in trouble, either way, I am happy because any other staff would have been calling our doctors right about now for approval to transfer one of us to the boys unit. Girls who touch other girls aren't going to touch boys, right? As Lubov wakes a sleepy Lia, I get up and walk into the kitchen area.

When I sit down at our table, the other Leah is already eating the limp noodles of a sickly macaroni and cheese dish that is passed around among us. My tray is unfortunately placed next to hers. With a mouth full of food, Leah begins blabbering on about her plan to get me a boy. Still feeling the weight of dreams, I hardly listen as Leah tells me that she wants to fix me up with Graham, a dork who looks like Macaulay Culkin with glasses. I am so not interested, but Leah continues explaining her plan. She says that since we only see the boys in the mornings at school, we will have to get Graham to shoot sperm then. Leah plans to distract Teacher Sam (the man who has us color pictures of buildings for edification) long enough for me and Graham to sneak under the counter like table in the back of our classroom and "do it." Even my half-hearted listening stops at this point because Teacher Sam is an oily man with a forward comb of dark mushroom hair, thin rimmed glasses and slick lips; Teacher Sam and the phrase "do it" should never be used in the same sentence. Eventually Leah asks me if I am listening to her and when I don't respond she gets bored and starts talking to Ashley who is sitting across from her.

After dinner we have night time activities, which include games of Pictionary and Scattergories. Then we have Check-out followed by bedtime snack. At Check-out we sit in a circle on the floor of the dark living room and talk about our day in three choppy sentences. Leah begins by turning to the staff members leading the circle and smiling, "Right now I feel happy. The high point of my day was eating nutritious food." She pauses for a pleased nod from staff and then continues, "And I didn't have a low point today; everything was great." I want to gag myself listening to Leah and I think Hannah feels the same way because I can tell she is biting her lip so hard she is about to break the skin. I push away the negative thoughts when it's my turn, "Right now I feel hopeful. The high point of my day was napping during shift change. The low point of my day was eating two boxes of cereal at snack." When the circle comes around to Lia her high point was napping too and she is feeling peaceful.

After eating an apple for snack, Lia brushes by me, sneaking a squeeze on my shoulder, and retreats to our room to change into her white hospital issue pajama bottoms and wait for me. Lubov is talking to us as she monitors our 45 minute snack period (15 minutes to eat, 30 minutes to sit after we eat). Although Lubov can't be older than 27, she is talking about the "old world" again. When someone has cut themselves, she has been known to say, "In old world we couldn't cut ourselves. Do you know why? If we cut ourselves in old world, we would get tetanus and our arms would fall off." When she says "old world," I think she is referring to Russia when it was The Soviet Union, but I've never asked to be sure. When the 45 minutes is over, we scatter and Lubov's "old world" is left behind.

I N OUR ROOM LIA is jumping up and down on her bed. She squeals as I enter the room and does a flip off of the bed. "I can fly," she says and begins to dance around me.

"Oh yeah," I ask playing along. "Like Peter pan?"

"Exactly!" She leaps over to the window and begins climbing on the ledge. She stands up and spreads her arms like wings and presses herself against the glass. "I'm going to jump out the window and fly into the night sky."

"What?"

She turns around to face me and starts jumping on the ledge, "I'm going to fly."

"You can't really fly. You know that, right, Lia?"

"Watch," She commands and she jumps onto my bed to ready herself for a running leap out the window.

I move backwards slowly, "I'm going to hit the nurse call button."

"No!" She screams and jumps from the bed tackling me to the ground then calmly states, "you can't do that."

"Lia, you can't fly. You will die if you jump out of the window."

"I'm immortal."

Reasoning with this girl who has the full weight of her body pressed against me isn't working, so I scream "Help, help!"

Lia takes one hand and clasps it over my mouth. With the other she pinches my nose closed and calmly whispers "Don't do that."

I try to push her hands away from my face and kick her off of me, but she is surprisingly heavy. Her hand is so tight on my mouth that she can't hear me say that I can't breathe. I have no choice; I bite her hand. Quickly releasing my face from her grasp, she laughs and springs upwards. She is headed for the window again; I scramble to my knees and grab her ankle. Lia falls to the ground with a hard thud. I climb on top of her and pin her down. She is laughing because it's all incredibly funny, but I'm about to start crying and screaming for help again when the door to our room opens and med nurse Patti comes to do her medicine rounds. Hearing Patti gasp at the sight of us on the floor, I jump off of Lia and frantically explain, "It's not what it looks like. She wants to jump out the window."

Still laughing, Lia corroborates my story, "I can fly."

Patti rushes to Lia, who is climbing the window again. Patti pulls her away and calmly escorts her to the door, "I'd really love to hear all about how you can fly. Let's get you calmed down, so you can tell me all about it." Lia waves her hand goodbye and I run to the door to watch as they disappear down the hall.

WHEN LUBOV COMES to do the first round of bed checks, I am sitting on the window ledge, watching the last bus of the night drive down Haste Street in the dark. Her voice startles me as she enters my room, "You know you've got your love riding on a dark horse." I snap my head in her direction and she continues, "Lia is Manic-Depressive, she's always going to be like this."

I shake my head fighting back tears. Lia is not always like that.

Lubov walks over and taps the glass on the window, "Plexiglas, it won't break. We're not going to let you girls hurt yourselves; you're safe in here."

I nod. I should have known that they wouldn't put actual glass in the windows when they took the doors off the closets in our rooms and they take our shoelaces and draw string pants.

"You know, in old world we can't stand still to be sad. Do you know why?" She pauses and waits for me to shake my head before continuing, "If we stand still too long in old world, we freeze to death."

I think she is trying to be funny, so I crack a small smile.

"Come, it's time to get in bed," she offers me her hand.

Taking her hand, I slide down from the ledge and crawl into my bed. Lubov pulls the covers up over me and thickly whispers, "sleep snug as a bug in a rug."

I'VE BEEN LYING in bed awake for at least an hour when Jude comes in to do morning vitals. She seems chipper and happy, strapping the blood pressure cuff to my left arm as I remain in bed. I am hardly as eager to start this day. After she pushes the button on the blood pressure machine and the cuff begins choking my arm, she slides a digital thermometer in my mouth for me to hold in place with my right hand. I turn my head and look at Lia's empty bed.

"She will be alright," Jude attempts to comfort me with all the information she is allowed to give and suddenly she doesn't seem all-knowing anymore.

She takes the thermometer out of my mouth a minute later and the blood pressure machine beeps. "Stand up slowly", she says, and I do. She sets the timer on the machine for two minutes and places two fingers above my left clavicle to measure my breathing while we wait. This is our morning routine.

When I don't say much Jude begins talking about the "amazing" movie we are going to watch after lunch, but I assume it's like the last educational movie we watched that put half of us to sleep, so I'm not listening. The blood pressure machine starts back up and Jude removes her fingers from my chest. When the machine stops she asks me if I am dizzy.

"No," I say and sneak a look at the final numbers. A 20 point heart rate increase is not enough to keep me in bed for the morning since my standing heart rate (I'm sure they have some sophisticated term for it) is still under 130 beats per minute, so Jude pulls the cuff off my arm and finds the key on her thick keychain to unlock my bathroom. I have 30 minutes.

As soon as Jude rounds the corner out of my room, Leah is standing in the doorway, "I heard your friend tried to off herself last night." Leah isn't supposed to be in my room, but she moves in and leans her arm against the bathroom door, "I can't believe there are people like her in here and they call us crazy."

"Get out!" I scream shoving Leah away from my bathroom.

She stumbles back a little and pretends to brush herself off with an innocent smile, "I was just coming to see if you wanted me to do your hair."

I stomp in the bathroom and slam the door. As I reach for the shower faucet, I hear Leah call, "You'll get in trouble for closing the bathroom door." I move to the sink while the water heats up. Stretching on my tippy toes, I reach above the light fixture to see if Lia has replaced the razor blade I hid from her last week; she has. As I turn to my distorted image in the thin slab of tin that is supposed to serve as a mirror, I take the blade and tear it across my hair. I am so sick of this tangled mess.

CELESTE GAINEY

in the days of early polyester

you don't know yet you are flammable;
jars of Miracle Whip, tubs of Polly-O in the fridge.
Your moral imperative on ice, the vertical blinds rattling shut,
sleek sofa of solid kerosene resisting your body's impression.
You keep saying, *Cotton, cotton, the touch, the feel of cotton,*
but you are drawn to the slinky boy shirt with the Kandinsky-like
print, fancy your stubbled side-burns whiskering
the top of its Byronesque collar—long points gesturing toward
no-tits torso, slim hips, bell-bottomed legs, Frye boots.
It feels like Velveeta against your skin, something you might
scrape off with the blade of your Swiss Army knife.
It seems to reject you. Still, you can't stop
parading your shirt through Washington Square Park
in the hot afternoon sun—looking for combustion.

CELESTE GAINEY

Best Boy

The chief assistant to the gaffer on a movie or television set.
There are no "best girls" per se. —IMDB Glossary

At the age of three
I tell my mother:
When I grow up, I'm going to be a man.
Like Pancho in *The Cisco Kid*:
high-heeled boots, a six-shooter.
Halloween, I'm a pirate with a hook,
in the Christmas pageant I insist on the Nutcracker
or Mouse King, never Marie.

Eighth grade, girls talk:
Who will get married? Make a good mother?
Not one can see me as a wife with kids.
It hurts a little to hear I'm not like them.
I'm a boy in a kilt and knee-socks—
When I grow up, I'm going to play the field.

In high school I meet a boy
I either love or want to be.
He wears madras shorts, crosses his legs elegantly,
holds his Winston like a lady.
One day in a crowded elevator as a joke
he yells *Fuck, fuck, fuck!*
All you ever want to do is fuck! Who do you think I am—Superman?
No, I say, *I'm Superman!*
You're Lois Lane.

Just out of film school,
I apply for membership in the Union.
All the Local 52 boss wants to know—
can I carry *horsecock* same as any man?
All I want to know—will he let me join his band of brothers,
be Best Boy—apprentice
to Vinnie Delaney, Milty Moshlak, Dickie Quinlan:
set their spider-boxes, haul their 4-aught,
flag their barn-doors, trim their brute arcs,
run their stingers, scrim their broads,
wrap their 9-light fays;
let them make me a man.

STACEY WAITE

Letter from Thomas Beattie to the Media
after Bassey Ikpi

This is me, pregnant, all man chest
and man chin, resting above a protruding
man belly, bursting with the burden of baby birth.

This is me, pregnant, feet strapped up
in stirrups at the obstetrician's, my legs
unshaven, my gender a *both-at-once*
in the face of fragile certainty.

There was a time you did not know me,
a time your safe sense of *this* or *that*
held you at night like an old blanket.
I do realize I've broken you.
I do realize I've sent you into a frenzy
of fortress protection.

But this is me, pregnant, carrying a life force
in my man body, pushing a baby through my
man-vagina, which I kept for such an occasion,
its hair coarse and thick with testosterone surge.

And you loathe me, even Oprah shifts in her chair:

> *But how could you…*
> *But how will you…*
> *But won't it be…*

This is me, pregnant, and there you are
with your *god made this*
and your *god made that.*

When what you really know when you see me
is that God made a pregnant man. You know
God made gender a fragile, silly thing. God made
gender a tire swing, some monkey bars.
God made gender an infinite playground.

This is me, pregnant, and I just might give birth
to a whole world, a whole nation of gender fuckers
rising out from my inevitable and impossible womb.

If Nancy Had an Afro

she'd use her bow
as a pick when it
gets too flat on one
side. If Nancy had
an afro, she'd dye
it blonde like Dietrich
shimmy like Aunt
flapper Fritzy, do
the Davy Jones
to a Madonna disco
tune. If Nancy
had an afro she'd ring
up RuPaul and lip
sync for her life, tear
it off, as bald
as Ongina. If
Nancy had an afro
Sluggo would want
dreads. Nancy has
a mad fro according
to Joe B. It spikes
like a porcupine
like tea or twinkle
lights a line
wrapped in black
and broken bulbs
an abandoned movie
house marquee

Sans Rhyme or Reason,
Mister Tries to Mind His Ps & Qs

Mister's martinis and clear mojitos
surprised no one last night least of all him.
Blame the full moon, blame the jukebox song list,
blame spring blossoming, but don't fault Mister,
that puppet of whacky gods, that lapdog
to screwball genes, that....
                              Three sheets to the wind,
Mister's mind dervished, imagination
poet and priest of late-night fantasies
that stared (*Tah-dah!*) a buffed Mr. Mister
and co-stared booze-boys-brawn commercial-free—
the 3 Rs of his MFA; the T
and bubble A of his 401 (K)
that's gorged now, its premium maturing;
the PBJ (*Yum!*) of his midnight snack.

MICHAEL MONTLACK

Running with the She-Wolf

Metal Bitch Barbara before her mirror
coated with hairspray and cigarette smog.
Denim Prophetess seeing much clearer
than I, her Prince Darling—poor kiss-less frog.

She powdered her cheeks, suburban gothic:
fully bedecked just to smoke in her yard.
Was this a duty as the town hot chick?
Her spikey galaxy: I the co-star.

Since everyone thought us the steamy pair,
no one intruded or bothered to ask.
I watched her each night layer make up and hair,
grasping the need for presentable masks.

My tough leather headbanger well hid the lace
only I glimpsed as she kept my straight face.

THOMAS GLAVE

Meditation (on "barebacking")

BECAUSE NOW THIS IS it, what we both want: me inside him, him inside me. What we want: to enter each other this way, completely unsheathed – "unprotected." To feel, really *feel*, the movements that some would term "dangerous," even "deadly": the sensation of ourselves moving through each other without fear. Without shame. Without (yes, at last, after so many years of so many warning messages, decades of Do-Not-Do-This-or-Ye-Shall-Pay-the-Dire-Price messages) worry. Without anxiety -- for the world with all its disapproval and warning is *out there*, we now tell ourselves, *so leave it behind. Forget about it. Yes, forget it,* he repeats to me, as, in this darkness that is utter secrecy and little more than breath and flesh, flesh and desire, I feel myself, an "outlaw" but truly free, now again rocking above him, pushing behind him; breathing in, out; moving into him now deeper, harder; my hands grasping his back; my arms reaching around to hold him closer; my mouth seeking again that part of his flesh (the taste of him still in my mouth, the width of his fully exposed length still filling my throat); my hand reaching down to steady myself inside him – inside him, just there, then there again, then even deeper, before the *And can*

we go even deeper? part that leads to the *Yes, of course, because* part...
which is exactly what I want, exactly the place I want so much to
be: where I am right now and wish to remain, without hesitation or
remorse, without warnings or scoldings as, a little later, or perhaps
sooner than I expect, I will feel him doing the same to me. For he too
will think and feel these things. He also will curl his lip at all those
remembered warnings about "safety" as, unimpeded by clear barri-
ers or the constant admonitions of Those Who Know Best, he will
move, rock, twist, and thrust in that place that is mine, his bare flesh
against mine: here, where, in secrecy, we can remain, but also become.
Remain together unmolested, at least for now. . . .Remain, our faces
turned toward each other's and occasionally away from each other's;
our faces sweating, perhaps spasming; our faces portraying, among
other words, the words "Yes" and "Yes, entirely," as, beyond here, we
disclose absolutely nothing to anyone of this union that is, because
of what and how it is, an "illicit" engagement; disclosing nothing to
any of the skulking frowners always outside, the knit-browed judges
ever present out there. The stalwart purveyors of the *Do Not* and *You
Should Not* rhetoric. Disclosing nothing to those who would tell us,
in those scolding tones, that we are being Bad Boys –Bad, yes, *because
you should not be doing this*, they will say yet again: *You really should
know better by now*, they will say, *for haven't we all lived and died with
It, the terrible thing, for well over twenty-something years now? Haven't
we learned? Haven't* you *learned? Don't you know that you should not
be so* (and then, as always, comes the dreaded word – the resented
word) Irresponsible?

   But then clearly some of these words, and the tone in which they
have been repeated to us over the years, form one of the irritations
here, vexations: years of being talked at and case-managed; years not
only of our having had to be "careful," but also of being commanded,
berated by The Authorities, to be so. Years of being told by The
Authorities that we are Bad because we might choose, for whatever
reasons (such as the pursuit of our particular intimacy, a need with its
own winding history), not to be "careful."   All the years of having to

navigate between obstacles to unimpeded closeness – the closeness we and others have craved for so long. And so perhaps partly in defiance of "reason" and everlasting caution (what tenacious caution, to abide not merely for years, but for decades!), here we are today and every day being Irresponsible, this man and me; being Irresponsible perhaps because we care deeply for each other, or maybe do not; but in any event doing exactly what we are doing right now because – well, for the simplest reason: because it feels *good*. It feels good unwrapped and gripped fearlessly in the hands, it brings actual bliss sliding uncovered between the teeth, and should I now tell you? Tell you how utterly amazing it feels to be able to say at last after years of **Be Safe** admonitions that here, at last, I am inside him without anything, anything at all wrapped around me, binding me. I am inside him without anything keeping him from feeling all of me, and he is, you are, *feeling* me in that deepest place from which now, holding onto me, pulling me down closer to you, into you, you wrench cries of *Jesus* and *God* as I move, *move* myself there in that place, your place, now completely unprotected, completely vulnerable, completely –

But yes. Exactly. Completely without shields.

Unshielded, as, soon, I know (and it is very important that I say this without shame), you will do it to me too. Haul me up, turn me around. Say to me, whisper, *Stay there. Yes, and relax*, you will say, while you – (but astonishingly slowly, in spite of the fervor that you feel), as I – (yes in exactly the way I have done so many times before). Everything in secret and perhaps – in fact definitely, without question – partly in defiance. In defiance because "This," we say to each other and might say to The Authorities one day soon if provoked enough, "This is what we want": not merely the being and moving inside, but what also looms for many as the truest danger in every sense: the releasing. The releasing at the moment of the gasp and shudder that makes for the quick heat that conjures "life," people say and believe, "life" – but life that, at least in our time, can also lead to death. Death so innocuously jetted between, or directly into, the place of solid muscles, and carried forward from there. Inward.

Yes, we know. For a very long time now, like countless others, we have known.

We know, and still are far from being the only ones. Far from being the only ones who yearn, in spite of all the risks, to move through each other without blockades. To move without guilt – for once without guilt! Guilt over being the despised "outlaw," and then survivor's guilt: recalling all those who fell along the way and still are falling, while we, in spite of all the risks, somehow did not fall, and have not fallen. *Not yet*, we do not say to each other – and, we hope, privately, not ever.

But then what about all the rest? – that is, the most frightening part? The part that murmurs, so quietly, Of course. Of course it is possible that, in spite of all he tells you and more, he might give It to you – as he fears, though also privately, that in spite of everything you have already said and not said to him – all assurances, promises and pledges of "the truth" openly uttered and tacit – you might give It to him. The possibility of "giving" in either direction a topic that, like a few other things, we have chosen not to discuss at length, as we remember that common sense and harsh reality are, more often than not, not enjoyable. As unenjoyable as uncertainty, anxiety; the lingering pall of distrust. And fear, of course – for always, no matter what we say nor what we feel, what we occasionally term "the enemy" – enemy of life, love, desire, and the uninhibited pleasure that is truest freedom – is never far away. It is a millstone never far from our movements public and private. Never far from our memory. Even if, as we might choose to believe, the enemy does not skulk directly between us, it always broods somewhere: *out there* somewhere and somewhere within: brooding and biding in the blood vessel; in the capillary that, so easily, unobtrusively, might rupture upon entry. We ponder these concerns now and again as (perhaps foolishly, even stupidly), determined to feel each other's *here*ness, we proceed into the practiced regularities of *relax, lie back* and *Of course, everything will be fine*: words we mouth to each other and ourselves. . .remembering that such words have accompanied untold others to efficient

and devastating communication of the enemy; to the disfigurings
of pain and tragedy, when all so many wanted was simply pleasure,
communion, and (yes, don't shrink away, *say* it!), what I wanted, what
I still want in spite of everything: love.

Love, without question. And so much more. And so now thinking
of love; thinking of you and how much I want to feel you and keep
you here beside me, inside me as I keep myself inside you where the
muscles grip tightest and move myself more deeply there and *there*,
I say again what we have never dared say aloud to anyone: that, in
this moment, I simply *do not care*. I do not care about all that we have
feared and continue to fear, because I am tired of all the enemy-laced
years. Exhausted from all the years of public service announcements
and precautions of Do not do this or that, Avoid contact with this,
and now make sure to don this carefully, so carefully, before you
ease in, before you permit the easing in. Remembering all that death
and shame and fear, but also so much yearning and desire, how can
I not say right now that with this man (you), or with another, with
someone, what I have always most deeply craved was, is. . .intimacy.
Closeness. Presence. Feeling. Touch. The joy and thrill of being seen,
and seen, wanted. Being wanted and found desirable, not at all easy
to experience in this world, not so common – *and so now more than
anything*, we say, you and I, *I want to feel myself inside you, completely
uncovered. Feel myself up against you as you thrust against me. Here,
where no one's brow will furrow in judgment and no one's lip curl in
scorn, I want to tighten my arms around you and tell you these things:
perhaps call you things like "beautiful one" or even "............" (the most
private name of all, never to be written). In this secrecy that blots out all
unwelcome things (including certain truths), we might finally believe that
desire and even love are. . . well, because everyone ultimately wants to
be desired and loved, loved somehow, isn't that right? That is what the
world tells us. That is what we seem to feel as human beings. It is what
popular songs and movies tell us we ought to want (though still mostly
only with the faces and voices of men and women saying these things to
each other – not too much, yet, with our kind, although it is beginning).*

If we do not admit that we want this and more – much more – we are kidding ourselves. Lying to ourselves. We know this, and in all honesty how could I not now admit that I am lonely without that intimate touch and the gaze that looks at me and actually sees. . .me. As I would like to see you. You who are sometimes beautiful, I would like to say, *gorgeous, in fact, and* (whether or not this is true) *mine. Mine,* I would love to say, *underneath me, or above, or somewhere in between. And I – yes, I could be yours in whatever way we choose to work it – for this moment or longer. And so give yourself to me. Open up and let me be there without interference. Without the obstacle of clear but durable barriers. Let me have an* effect *on you and make you remember me. Let me look at you and feel that I have touched you irrevocably in the most receptive place imaginable, and that now, more than ever – not only because of this, and because of so much more – you feel that way about me. As I – as you –*

But the truth is that I have no idea at all what will happen next. Nor does he. Nor might any of the other hes who may or may not traverse this terrain. I have closed my eyes. We have closed our eyes. Closed our eyes in part to the past – a past that gradually, amid laughter, discovery, love, and suffering, became terrible, unbearable, splotched by purple marks and relentless mutating encroachments. Splotched by shallow breathing, the thick scent of lilies, and the inhibition – corruption – of pleasure. Today, in the secret place and beyond it, we only know that the future, like death, like the most unforeseen outcome of risk, is unknowable. Today, at least, there will be no room for the publicly encouraged "good"-ness; no quarter for the commonly demanded "responsibility"; no place – not here, certainly – for the generally expected "maturity." Today, at least, life, joy, power, vulnerability, recklessness, desire, and perhaps the possibility of love and closeness (or at least the prospects of wanting and being wanted, coupled with intense affection), loom. By way of the words that will later lead us to those deeper corridors of our dreams, the dream, we know now that, through these moments, our eyes remain closed, screwed tightly shut as, feeling this, then feeling that and that again, we shudder because he (you) will not let me go. *I will not let him go. Because now he is holding that part of me before his face and breathing it in. Because now, utterly unprotected, he is trembling and gasping beneath me, above me, calling out my name. He whispers it, shouts it, as I hold on to his hair, as he holds my hair, as we are not safe, no, in no way are we being safe. For there is, can be, no safety here, we both laugh. Anywhere. And so all right then, we say without saying it: Let it all remain a secret. One that we will never tell anyone, not this time nor when it happens again. For it will, we know, happen again. And again. But for now, we will keep silent, both of us, as we begin to dream. Dream of how, together, we are completely inside, unseen, where none of the others will ever find us. Where no one can stop us. Neither stop nor prevent us, my love, about which I promise – yes, to you I truly do promise – I will never, ever tell.*

A Joyful Noise

Rubbing against the music minister after the first day of the
Billy Graham crusade in Atlanta, I silently counted youth group
members counting on me to keep the promise made to come
back with beer. I always came back with something for the other
northwest Florida teens who took a chance on me with their
tithing change, our sack of quarters along the front pocket of
my tan corduroys, pants on the floor of the van of the Woodpine
Presbyterian Church, my underwear in the hands of the man
who directed the choir, now directing me: on my knees, open my
throat, watch my teeth, and sing. Later the group would convince
me I was the greatest, loading our dormitory bathtub with ice to
keep the can beer cold. I was old enough to almost get away with
it, but late for the next morning's hymns. I was strong enough to
stand the punishment – 24-hours under the lock and song of our
chaperone, which meant sharing his bedroom. I was counting on
the two more nights till we got home.

No Better

The young kid who lives next door
just called his dog a faggot.
His voice is about to change. I can hear it
on the cusp of deepening. I wince,
think: I am a faggot. I really like his dog.
I imagine a different version
of me, the one who goes onto the porch,
asks him not to say that, although I know
it's likely the word of choice for a 9th grader.
Another other version of me
goes onto the porch, says Dude, I'm a homo.
Knock it off. Another version
goes into his yard, cracks him
in the mouth backhanded, tells him
not to be so ignorant. I can imagine him
at the same junior high I was so miserable in,
at the lockers near the gym, boys slapping each other,
saying things to say them. His dog is fluffy
and golden, licks me when I go to my car. The kid
has helped me shovel snow, always says hi,
much nicer than his twat of a miserable sister.
Maybe his dog is a homo, who knows,
but I know when he said faggot he meant
asshole or motherfucker just as I mean
asshole or motherfucker when I yell
from inside my car at the buttfucker
who cuts me off.

Henry Miller, Anais Nin, John Updike, Philip Roth and others write about sex with their HIV-positive lovers ending with lines by from Sappho*

I lose what words I have.
I unbuttoned her pants,
took his penis in
my jeweled hands.
The lightest teasing
of the tip
makes a fire run
beneath my skin.

My penis
at present arms.
Her sex
a giant hothouse flower
like blood-red camellias,
opened by force.

He wants to lie down
on the floor or
she wants my pussy
in her magnificent mouth or
he pushes Drake's Daredevil
cupcakes down over my cock
and then eats them off me,
flake by flake.

She put her legs around my neck.
The dance hall,
the money rhythm,
the love that comes over the radio,
her body.

She pours maple syrup
out of the Log Cabin can.
Sweat pours from me
and trembling takes my body whole.
I slid in
 "Get it in" she said.
I slid in
"all the way" he said.
I slid in like a cloud
in a dream.

Her body began churning
like a bump and grind dancer
running to points of brilliance,
like bells rippling up
and up exquisite,
exquisite and melting
her all molten inside

like soft flames,
twitching and fluttering,
a sacrament
from a lascivious angel.
"God," he said. "I can't stop it."

I lose what words I have.
A fire runs beneath my skin.
Sweat pours from me
and trembling
takes my body whole.
And yet I'll dare it,
just a little more.

*The line "I fear I too will die" is omitted.

MIGUEL MURPHY

Coprophilia

Pick now the plump
gold snail of a woman's, ashen

white as god & steaming

still on the immortal sky-
clear glass table her husband lay
beneath. He wanted

to see *it* happening, this soft

perverse remedy for burns & it once
was thought, for breast cancer.

He wanted to watch
nightmare's mouth
scatalogically

blossoming. He lay under it,
the table, & when he saw the devil's

eye-mouth open she could hear him moan

coo & baa, because we do—
when sickness takes its whip-
slap out, we do—lie there & struggle

moonhowling *no* for *yes*

as if heartache had a cure. As if
           one clothespin pinched onto a nipple's
pink moon, as if the sight of one purple-hooded
           daub

pierced straight through, weren't enough. One silver
              perfect cockring, one threatening
black leather mask, military's
           degradation

           catcalling. One blind
    erotically tall boot—unlaced & St. Andrew's
            Cross, passion's torture-wheel. It's true
the science of love is in

           our blood—fetish
satisfies, redeems, pinks itself, penetrates & sacrifices
            truth to the scrutiny of others, yields
to shame

           to prove itself, disarms & offers
& dares. Even Nature's
           scat mixes in

           to gentle unguents, excrement's

crass miracle. Dirty salve. And if by crying
           he meant to fake, to imitate the symptoms
of saintly ecstasy & pain, this man
                palpitating under his wife's rank

reliquary load, under her golden
            pile of defilements, this

    man staring hard at
the rose of her opening
            above him, watching her squat

on the table for a moment, breathing
            slowly as the coiled & bronzed
defecations pearl out—

he is like us, who in our private

feasts also want
            to answer death, who also
want to cure ourselves
            psychosomaticizing epileptic

fits, fevers & headaches
            & jaundice, meaning, we see
in ourselves the animal

world, meaning, save us, *O bestial*
            affection: oh dog, and *ah* dove,
and—it's sinister, but—*oh*
            goat, *save us.*

Bastard

Ten yrs old   eyes shiny like crude oil
used to wonder who
supplied these endless eyes

But clearly   was you
rotten vision not inherited   instead
conditioned
        weekends locked in
        basement   bedroom
reading   (no other choice)
Treasure Island   *The Hardy Boys*   *Nancy Drew*
over over   over past
stung ray'd eyes   past
saltwater (mourning tears
for Mom's
        buried eyes)
past uglypity   palerage
for letting new bride   (merciless beauty)
win
prizing those eyes that
should have been   watching me
then the youngest

        instead

a career
        in solitude
started   so by fifteen
when sent away
        "emancipated" (the law calls it)

by stepmom's plot of perjury   ("attempted murder")
      that Port Authority desertion
      only
embellished could-have-but-never-gaves:
eyeglasses   driving lessons   birthday candles

32   still a bastard   that boy still spills into this face
that why you passed
not recognizing   eyes you made?
I've traded books for   dvd marathons
aisle seats in movie theatres
      w/out company
not having to speak/care
      un-anguished
but now   here
asked you to talk   yet
I've been littering
parts of speech   like
cigarette butts   because
how   why
interrogate about
      abandonedthingspast   (this time, meaning you)

I remind you my bland name   again

but meant to say:

"Dad" (a formality)
can you bear to see
how

        ruthlessly
        and unfinished

I do
pardon
you?

—for Aaron Bonventre

SAEED JONES

Prelude to Bruise

In Birmingham, said the burly man –

Boy, be
a bootblack.

Your back, blue-black.
Your body,   burning.

    I like my black boys broke, or broken.
    I like to break my black boys in.

See this burnished
brown leather belt?
You see it, boy?

    Are you broke, or broken?
    I'm gonna break your back in.

Good boy. Begin: bend
over my boot,

    (or I'll bend you over my lap – *rap, rap*)

again, bend. Better,

butt out, tongue out,
lean in.

    Now, spit shine.
    Spit polish.

My boot, black.
Your back, blue-black.

Good boy.
Black boy, blue-black boy.
Bad boy – *rap rap*.

You've been broken in.
Begin again, bend.

MONICA CARTER

Seven Truths of a Woman

T HE WOMAN MAKES HER LOVER scrambled eggs with garlic and mushrooms. The lover, of medium height and well-defined muscles, tan with light brown hair, eats them while she reads the paper. The lover kisses the woman and promises to call her later. Don't forget to lock the door on the way out, the lover says.

GREED

The woman is alone in her lover's apartment. The smell of garlic is in the kitchen. The smell of sex is in the bedroom. The woman looks through the lover's mail to see where the lover spends her money, what she likes to read and who she wants to save. The woman turns on her lover's computer to see what programs she uses to entertain herself, to make her life easier, to keep things private. The woman, a generous three inches shorter than the lover, opens her closet and looks at the shoes she wears, feels her shirts, peers into the boxes above.

LUST

The woman finds her lover's pictures. The woman stares at the lover's cream colored teeth and large breasts with her arm draped around another woman who looks much like herself. That woman, the ex-girlfriend in the picture, is blonde and curvy, petite with delicate hands and peach painted nails. The woman commits to memory the lover's family. The lover gazes back from the glossy pictures and asks her silently what she is doing there, staring at her past? The woman snaps the album shut and her hand strokes the light blue long-sleeved shirt the lover wore the first time they met. She opens the album again and fingers the sharp corners, devouring the faces, figuring out what part of her lover's heart these people occupy.

ANGER

Later that afternoon sitting at her own kitchen table, the woman checks her phone. Her apartment smells of cinnamon candles, not of sex or garlic. The lover leaves a message saying that she would like to see her this weekend. The woman cries because the weekend is three days away and that is three days of cinnamon.

SLOTH

For three days, the woman watches television. The woman lies on her couch, flashes of television colors poking at the darkness. The woman leaves her laundry dirty, leaves her dishes in the sink and watches as boxes crackers and cereal disappear from her cupboard. On the third day, the woman counts the piles of crinkly balls of Kleenexes that are scattered throughout her one-room apartment. There are nine piles. Later she finds one in the bathroom that she missed. She does not bathe.

ENVY

The woman decides to call her friend, the one with a live-in girl-friend. The woman listens to the friend's happiness, her voice's highs and seductive lows. The friend tells the woman that she is in love. The woman doesn't want her friend to be happy. She wants her friend to be dirty, sitting in the dark, and counting piles of Kleenex like she is. She tells her friend that the girlfriend won't last.

GLUTTONY

The lover smiles when she sees the woman walking into the restaurant wearing black stockings, black pumps and vintage earrings. The lover recalls the moist surrender when she touched this woman in her intimate places. The woman and the lover, they eat passionately with their mandibles gnawing and their teeth pulling meat from the bones followed by hearty swallows of red French table wine. After they leave the restaurant, the woman climbs on top of the lover before she starts the truck. The lover and the woman suck and pull at each other's lips and tongues just as hungrily as they had eaten their meat earlier. The woman and the lover make each other rock and release before the lover turns the ignition. They, the woman and the lover, return to the lover's apartment where they do this three more times before morning because that's what the woman wants.

PRIDE

The woman makes the lover scrambled eggs with garlic and mushrooms as she did a few days before. The woman cleans the heavy cast iron skillet and wipes the counter. The lover comes up behind her and envelops the woman's waist with her muscular arms. The lover asks the woman what she would like to do that day. The woman pulls away, gives her a passive smile and tells her that she would like to go home.

REDEMPTION

That very night, the woman, she, goes to a bar wearing the same black stockings, the stockings stained with last night's lusty impatience, wearing the same black heels the heels that cuddled next to each other on the lover's dusty floorboard, and she finds a someone.

Not a lover, but an other. The other is appointed a job for that evening that she does not know about—she is the savior.

T HE WOMAN TAKES the righteous healer to her one room apartment, where the lover has never been, and feels the tongue of vindication lap at the walls of the woman's guilt. There are pictures in the woman's mind, photographs she would like to put on display. Shiny color photographs of the smiling lover and the woman sealed under glass waiting to be broken. She thinks about these framed pictures that will never be on her nightstand as the healer prods and licks her deep inside where the woman hides her fear. The healer savors the fear on the tip of her tongue as if she tastes the sour aftertaste of ecstasy. But the woman does not think of ecstasy. Instead, she sees splashing rays of whiteness suffocating her thoughts of the lover and as the woman holds her breath, purity rolls through her memory and for one sightless instant, this woman feels absolution.

ABBIE J. LEAVENS

Ledges

You were scared to merge
and semis—they scared you too,
but you drove my car
to your town anyway

The park was flooded, so we
ordered two beers—

I wasn't ever sorry

We wouldn't touch the radio
only touched each other
and listened

       That man passing, and
that woman
       paisley drunk and unloved

       sounds from the bar spilling into the street
         you further in me than ever before

MAUREEN SEATON

Cradle of Life
Letters to my daughter from South Florida, 2003

It's only what drives you more and more openly
to suicide that saves you . . .
        —Walter Lowenfels, *Letters to an Imaginary Daughter*

I took Lori to see Lara Croft for her birthday today and my favorite
part was when Angelina flew in her parachute outfit and landed
feet first on a boat. If I ever found the Cradle of Life, I'd walk
away from the fortune and keep going until I hit the mangrove
swamp. Outside the theater was a makeshift barnyard in honor of
another movie, Seabiscuit, which made little sense since there were
no horses present. I couldn't watch the kids poke the goats and
ducks, so Lori took me home and here we are, waiting for the
drawbridge on Dania Beach Boulevard. Lori turned 49 today and
said she wants to have her 50th birthday in Far Rockaway at her
mother's house, and I got really sad because I'll be leaving Lori
before she turns fifty, although she doesn't know this yet and
neither do I.

Before the movie I saw a woman on the ticket line who lives down
the street from us. She walks to the beach everyday, stays there
a long time with her friends, then walks back to her condo. She
has very short hair and is thin, the way I would like to be, but
instead I get to sit and write poems. That's my theory. She smiled
and waved to me, something she'd never done before. If I had a
beautiful body, which I did for exactly three months once when
you were eight years old, I might be a bathing beauty too. Not that
I don't like using my mind. It's a good consolation prize. But when
I chose which I wanted more, good body or brain, I don't think I

was properly informed about where I would be living one day
or who my neighbors would be. You can tell I kind of rushed
through the orientation, grabbing cookies as I headed for door #2.

Last week someone died in a jet-ski accident and I thought of that
today during Lara Croft because Angelina Jolie and her double
were showing off on a jet-ski. When I was a musician I used to
worry about my hands, what I would do if I ever lost or injured
them, plus, how would I type? Which is what I'm doing right
now, typing some crazy stuff in Florida as you do the same a
thousand miles away in Chicago. Malcolm just meowed until
I yelled at Lori to feed him—not yelled yelled, just loudly through
the back door so she could hear me. She's 49! By all rights, having
had her arm almost completely severed one time and having
fallen halfway through two moving subway cars another, she
should be dead. Yet here she is, nodding in the heat and waiting
for Chinese food, which is what she wants for her birthday
celebration. I offered to take her out anywhere, but I think she was
influenced by the movie, which took place partly in Shanghai. She
leaned over and whispered, Where's Shanghai?

Now there's a scuba diver in the turquoise part of the sea. He's
underwater, searching for the Cradle of Life. I read that it's hotter
in Chicago in July than it is in Miami, and since I've lived in both
places I know this to be true. The other day I got seasick from
floating on my back in a totally calm sea. I've gotten seasick in
the backs of cars, on airplanes, on waterbeds, and in a flotation
tank in Chicago that was meant to reduce sensation and bring me
to my higher self. Apparently, my higher self needs Dramamine
The temperature of the sea in Miami is almost as high as the
air—87 degrees. In Chicago, Lake Michigan only makes it to 65.

I forgot to say that the average high for July in Chicago is 95 degrees and the high for Miami in July is 92 degrees. It gets hotter in Chicago in July but not for very long. Remember the year several died in the heat up there? Melters. They say that people make jokes to feel better. When Lori and I went to the Everglades we took a boat tour and hit a huge electrical storm. Lori sang the theme from Gilligan's Island and everyone laughed. She herself laughs at every opportunity. I've seen people cross over into hysteria around Lori quite easily. I keep telling her she could do stand-up or run for office. The Cradle of Life mostly exists in movies and books, although I got close to it once in Wyoming. The scuba diver is gone now, his little yellow flag no longer bobbing up and down. He must have left the sea while I wasn't looking. Like the day there were three manatees heading north about a hundred yards out and I had my back to the ocean, working on my tan. That day my thin neighbor and her friends ignored me as usual and Lori was asleep back at the house. Some guy tapped me on the shoulder and said: If I were you, I'd turn around.

Siberia

He is driving. His hand moves to my knee.
While he chats about his life in Russia,
I stare at the red patch on his knuckle.
It's cold as Siberia, I mention.

He describes the weather in Russia
as I roll up my window, turn on the heat.
It's not that cold in Siberia—I'm corrected,
nervous that it's contagious

as he rolls up his window, cranks up the heat.
I stare at the red patch on his knuckle.
Don't worry, he says, It's not contagious.
He is driving. His hand is on my knee.

STEPHEN ZERANCE

The Night Watch

I hunt in the mirror for a scare
inside my mouth, the first white
spot on the back of my throat, checking
if my gums have receded from the teeth
in high arches, for tenderness
in the neck, armpits, and groin,
a colorful blotch on the back of my thigh,
on my feet—between the toes. The lint
from a black sock shocks me.

I am six, finishing a nightly bath.
I do not unplug the drain. I decide
to bob face down on the water,
to fake I am drowning.
I dip my head under, closing my eyes,
turning my head to the side.
I float. My breath makes dents in the water.
I wait for my father to come up the stairs.

DAVID TRINIDAD

AIDS Series

1.

I met Larry Stanton at a party on the Lower East Side, Indian
summer, 1982. My maiden trip to New York. Nervous and unsure
of myself, pinned against the wall in a room full of poets,
cocktail chatter, cigarette smoke. I'd just lit a Marlboro Light
when Larry, part of the small group I was trying to converse
with, leaned forward and kissed me on the lips. That's all I
remember. He might have invited me to visit his studio; Tim
might have taken me there. He might have come to my reading
at St. Mark's. I only remember that mysterious kiss. And his
looks: a boyish blond who had morphed into an unkempt mid-
thirties handsomeness. I open the book of his paintings to a self-
portrait he did in 1984, the year he died. He stares back, sad and
cute. It aches to look into his face.

2.

Lee Hickman and I became friends in the early eighties, after
he published me in *Bachy*. Peter Cashorali (another young
Los Angeles poet Lee had published) and I would hang out
with him, ask him burning questions about poetry. Lee was
dismayed that he couldn't give away a perfectly good copy of
Pound's *Cantos*—nobody wanted it, Peter and myself included. I
accompanied him to San Francisco (where he gave a reading); on
the way back he got a speeding ticket outside of Santa Barbara.
For his birthday I gave him a pair of elegant champagne flutes.
He showed me a letter Anne Sexton had sent him, praising his
poem "Lee Sr Falls to the Floor." It was confusing when Lee
rejected all the local poets he had supported and took up with
the Language poets: he seemed angry for some unknown reason,

acted like he wanted to punish us. One day when I was at Astro's
with Bob and Sheree, Lee came in and sat at the counter. My book
Monday, Monday had just come out; I had one with me and
debated whether I should give it to Lee. Bob and Sheree
encouraged me. I walked over and offered it to him: "I hope you
enjoy it." Several weeks later, he showed up at a reading and asked
me to sign the book I'd given him, on the last page of my poem
"Meet The Supremes." I wrote: "Lee, where did our love go?"

3.

I went to Astro's with Glen after one of my first A.A. meetings,
fall of 1983. Chain-smoked and drank countless cups of coffee.
Glen was loud and funny and overweight. I could do little but
listen. I've never forgotten something he said that night: "Even
a bowel movement can be spiritual." I didn't—and still don't—
know what he meant. He gave me my *Big Book*, wrote in it:
"David T., May you have many sober years, Glen." His gesture
and message made a difference: I've been sober nearly three
decades. Early on, Glen celebrated a "birthday" at the Hollywood
Squares meeting on New Hampshire. All of the celebrants stood
in line to blow out candles (one for each year of sobriety) on a cake
and address the crowd. The man in front of Glen carried his toy
poodle with him. When it was his turn, Glen walked up to the
podium and said, "I always knew if I got sober, I'd follow a dog
act."

4.

I was a year and a half sober when I saw Steve at an A.A. meeting.
He had three or four months. I couldn't understand why I found
his profile so captivating; that had never happened before. A
psychic confirmed that it signified a past life connection. A sense
of stoic intensity, like T.E. Lawrence. Late twenties. Thinning

blond hair. Wore a black-and-white kaffiyeh wrapped around
his neck. Estranged (because he was gay) from his family in
Albany, New York. In his living room in Pasadena, we slow
danced to Carly Simon's "The Right Thing To Do" then laid on his
couch and kissed. When he ran his index finger up and down
my wrist, I thought of the Ted Hughes line "Under the silk of
the wrist a sea." When we moved to Simple Minds at an A.A.
dance, he smiled and mouthed, "Don't You Forget About Me."
When things became emotionally fraught, my A.A. sponsor
insisted I break it off: it was too soon for Steve to start dating.
"Maybe when he has more time. . . ." When I told Steve we
needed to wait, tears literally flew out of his eyes. After he left,
I sat on the floor under my Isermann clock and cried. Before he
moved home to Albany (where he would die), we talked on the
telephone. He told me how angry he was at me. For once, I didn't
get defensive, just let him have his feelings. I'm happy that I
was able to respond tenderly. What bothers me is that I can't
remember Steve's last name.

5.

Ron Cahill was a friend my last year in Los Angeles. We met
through Sally, an overbearing woman we both knew from the
program. In our early conversations, we tried to make sense of
Sally's personality. There was a sadness about Ron—pushing
forty, positive, no relationship, fed up with the West Hollywood
scene. I've sometimes thought that, under different circumstances,
we might have been boyfriends. I still have the copy of Capote's
Answered Prayers he gave me for Christmas 1987, inscribed with
red ink: "Love, Ron." After I moved to New York, we kept in
contact: there are twelve letters and eighteen postcards from him
in my papers at NYU. I regret that I was standoffish when he sug-
gested a visit; I was swamped with graduate work. He was hurt.

His postcards mentioned that he was on a regimen of Chinese herbs, and was considering moving to Texas to be close to his family. Then an abrupt message from Sally on my answering machine: Ron was dead. No details, no number to reach her. Years later, when she found me through the Internet, I told her how her message left me stranded with the news of Ron's death, how difficult that had been for me. Her reply was curt: "You poor thing."

6.

A few weeks after I arrived in New York, Raymond Foye took me to lunch with Cookie Mueller, Vittorio Scarpati, and John Wieners. An Indian restaurant in the East Village. I was seated across from Wieners, who was certain he'd encountered me in Canada years before. Every time I'd try to converse with him, he'd first say something coherent, then lapse into incomprehensible utterances. I don't remember talking with Cookie at all. When the waiter brought out our food, he dropped the huge silver tray just as he reached our table. We waited while the meal was prepared a second time.

7.

I liked Karl Tierney and I liked his poems, but all I can remember is that in the restaurant in San Francisco where we ate, our booth had a curtain.

8.

Amy said that when she visited Tim Dlugos at Roosevelt Hospital in 1989, he was reading *Our Mutual Friend*, Dickens' last novel, a book he'd been reading, off and on, since at least 1981. I think she said there were yellow flowers in the room. Eileen said that when she visited him a year later, during his final hospitalization, Tim was trying to eat pink yogurt, but his lips were too swollen. The radio was on a local station playing "Ruby" songs: "Ruby Baby," "Ruby Tuesday," "Ruby, Don't Take Your Love To Town." Jane said that at the end Tim was on so much morphine it seemed he was in a coma. She held his hand or sometimes, exhausted, laid forward with her head and arms in the bed. Even slept. "It was very peaceful to be with him." For years I lamented the fact that I wasn't able, as he was dying, to talk with him about what was happening. It would have felt intrusive for me to bring it up. Eileen said she just held Tim's hand and told him she loved him. That was helpful to hear. The next time I visited him on G-9, I did the same. Tim said, "I love you, too." It was late afternoon, and we sat, mostly in silence, as the light faded. I remember everything as gray.

9.

Joe Brainard was so sweet and polite, so self-effacing, it's hard to summon many specifics. I do remember that when he came to a dinner Ira and I gave, he drew the face of a troll doll in our guest book. And that he flipped over *A Class Apart*: Montague Glover's photographs of soldier boys and rough trade, their large penises showing through trousers and bathing suits. And that he was once sitting in Aggie's, a restaurant that used to be on the corner of West Houston and MacDougal, when I walked by. I didn't see him, but he saw me. "I saw you!" he said, the next time we were together. He mentioned it two or three times after that: "I saw you!" It seemed so significant to him. "I saw you!"

zubat

we are the living emblem of coupling
unsure of what it means
to be sad in the twenty-first century
will not recognize anybody
has the right to possession that does not
include the right to bear a body
in dark light of sunday edging
cusp of a day by a different name
and from the bridge they will emerge
ahaze with rolling black wings
like the skyline is now a lava lamp
but maybe we will not look
maybe we will stay
committed to the grass and occasional
dirty stare from a conservative jogger
until there is no one on congress
and something inside us
will whisper it is monday morning
though morning seems a misnomer
because the moon is prime
and then i might kiss you
in a funny place like your nose
and if you are awake i will tell
you how much it means to me
to access such a time of day
an hour
i have slept through my whole life.

ERIN ROTH

How to Be a Dyke: A Primer

ON POSTURE

There was something about the way she walked. I was fifteen and had just come out to myself, so I didn't recognize it as a lesbian walk, but my body recognized it as a mysteriously compelling way to move. Through careful observation I noted the idiosyncrasies of it- she stepped heavily each foot, without shifting her weight from side to side, she kept her hands in her pockets, elbows out, and – the most telling detail of all – she carried her books at her side, supporting their weight with her hand, not cradled up in her arm and pressed against her chest like all the other girls did. I chalked it up to her being foreign, because I was in high school in a small, white, blue-collar town and figured that not being American could lead to all kinds of ailments, not the least of which was a strange way of walking.

The girl with the strange walk was an exchange student from Germany, and she joined my Girl Scout troop a few months into the school year. She began to assimilate into my group of friends, charming everyone with her accent and her short stature. We teased her about her "soccer walk" and her nationality, and I regarded her with interest and curiosity.

Whatever compelled me to reveal to her the sexuality I was still so insecure with, I will never know for certain. But I will guess it had something to do with that walk.

I showed her a note I had written about some girls I thought were pretty, a note with sexual overtones. She read it and found me in the tiled high-school cafeteria later that day, her eyes hungry.

"I am the same way." Her English was spectacular, although her phrasing was sometimes strange. "I can't believe, I mean, I didn't know…" We giggled about it awkwardly, and later that same day she passed me a folded note she had written in study hall.

"I thought I would come to America and forget about this," she wrote on the lined graph paper she brought from home.

We began passing notes every day. I would hand her one before homeroom, and she would give me one back at 4th period. I'd write a reply in study hall and hand it to her after school. After a while the note-writing became pointless, because we would spend most of our evenings together, at Scouts or in Wilderness Club after school or hanging out at my house. Eventually we spent every night together, after her host-sister was arrested for shoplifting and her parents asked their exchange student to move out for a while so they could "handle things". By this point she had already kissed me, first in the back of the public library, then again at the top of my staircase, then again everywhere else we went away from adult eyes. We had already held hands down the bunny hill as she taught me to ski and stayed late at school while I showed her how to paint. She had already unhooked my bra and silently fucked me in her host family's spare bedroom in the trailer park. So when they kicked her out, my mother took her in, thinking she was helping out her daughter's best friend.

She told me she loved me one morning in May, and moments later my mom hollered upstairs that pancakes were ready. We sat across the table from each other while I tried to force syrupy pancakes into my storming stomach and she made eyes at me over the butter. She added "forever" to the sentence by the end of the month, while we were on our weekend camping trip with Wilderness Club, zipped into our double-wide sleeping bag in our little one-person tent. Somewhere in the depths of Algonquin Park, Ontario, she carved our initials into a young tree by the water.

She went back to Germany in July, but she didn't cheat on me until September. It was, suddenly, over with the girl with the strange walk. I was almost sixteen and officially a lesbian.

IDEOLOGIES

High School:

"Yeah, my girlfriend and I were making out by our lockers after school and some teacher came over and told us to stop. It was so unfair, I felt really persecuted," says the girl with dreadlocks to the Queers and Allies meeting.

On a Date:

"Oh my god, isn't this place so cute?" The girl I had made out with the night before is referring to the expensive and obnoxiously modern ice cream shop we are in. "These are exactly the kind of chandeliers I want in my house, when I have that much money."

At a Party:

A dark-haired Filipino girl is taking a drag from her cigarette in the backyard of a college house party, her arm wrapped around the waist of a tall brunette. "I guess I'm officially off the market this coming Saturday, so we're having a bachelorette thing." She's not getting married, she's planned the day they are going to start dating.

Sophomore Year:

I'm sitting in someone's house because they're having a "lesbian party", whatever that means, and the girls across from me are making out heavily while someone screams across the room that we should make this a no-shirts party.

In the Dorms:

"But he is so nice to you, and you guys get along so well!" I am arguing with my bisexual roommate over the wonderful man she refuses to date. "He's just..." she thinks it over. "He's so into sports and...I just don't want to be in such a straight relationship, that's all."

My Last Q&A Meeting:

"The people fighting for marriage equality are making it worse for everyone by buying into the same heteronormative bullshit, they are just trying to tack 'gay' onto 'white-male-privileged'," says the pangendered activist to the college Queers and Allies meeting.

To All Of It:

Fuck these people, I think.

APPEARANCES

Nicole was the first love of my life. I spent most of ninth grade writing bad poetry about her rose-scented hair and almond-shaped eyes. It took the exotic touch of a German lesbian to push her out of my mind, but after we broke up she crawled back in. She was strangely shaped, with wide hips and a small chest and a lanky, stretched figure. Shortly after I'd turned sixteen, we made out for the first time in her king-sized bed covered in pink pillows and stuffed animals. Our making out transitioned gradually into sex over the next two years.

She had been my best friend since seventh grade. All of my begging and pleading with her had not made her fall in love with me when we were fourteen, but now she was sixteen and had still never been kissed, and I was no longer in love with her, so the timing was perfect. I broke down crying every few weekends in the middle of a makeout session, bogged down with the guilt of my mother's hatred for my newly-announced sexuality, but I managed to get over that by the start of our senior year. We spent that year alternately fingering each other quietly in her bedroom and fighting loudly in the hallway at school.

We told only two people about our relationship. I told my ex-girlfriend in a successful attempt to wound her, and another friend's younger sister who followed me around with hopeful puppy eyes, hoping to let her down easy and knowing she worshiped me too much to tell anyone. Barring these exceptions, no one knew, ourselves included, that we were dating.

No one would have suspected her for a dyke. She was pretty with long brown hair and dark eyes, a fondness for stilettos and red lipstick. I was a bespectacled nerd with cropped red hair and a collection of baggy T-shirts with slogans like "When all the trees are burned, you'll learn you can't eat money." On her own, she attracted some guys, but turned them down for a hundred different reasons all stemming from her own fear. Being attached to me all the time turned her into the talk of the town, because everyone knew how I was. She counteracted this by becoming increasingly feminine and somehow increasingly more dependent on me, until the summer after high school, when she found a boy she could stand and fucked him. Then we went to college and she found another boy, and fucked him, and then another after that. I went to college and told everyone about her, so that when she came to visit me everyone saw her as my lesbian ex-girlfriend. She, on the other hand, told no one at all about me. Today she is still my best friend – my pretty, straight, well-dressed best friend.

THE USE OF ALCOHOL

Lesbians should not drink alcohol. It was a realization I came to junior year of college when I drowned in it, too absorbed in my bottomless capacity for love and my inability to find it to crawl out of my depression. This is not, of course, a problem unique to lesbians. But the combination of endless self-pity and overly dramatic love lives leads to a belief that your ability to feel, to emote, is so much greater than that of your peers that no one could ever understand you.

There were plenty of cute lesbians at school, but they each had a strike against them. This one was too much of a stoner, that one was a player, this one was homely and large and I was, quite frankly, a bit of a bitch. All I wanted was for someone to pin me to a wall in the dark corner of a party and make me forget that I was destined to die, the only thing I had thought about for months. It had been a constant source of anxiety for me since I was a kid; I felt, more acutely than most other people seemed to feel, the constant nagging of my mortality and the bleak nothingness that awaited me. When I had been with a girl that feeling had lessened, sometimes had even disappeared completely. Dykes have a way of emotionally complicating every relationship to the point that things like death pale in comparison, and I needed that anger, that jealousy, that passion and that sex to forget my ultimate fear.

It had been two years since I had had a real relationship, and in that time I had kissed two people – one, my ex-girlfriend when she came to visit, and two, a stranger in a dark, sweaty dance club. In the light of day we went on a date and I realized she had a big mouth and showed too much gum, so the following semester I retreated back into the dark corners of clubs and party houses. I started off the semester with a slightly overweight girl who had professed an interest in me; then, a slim girl who smelled of smoke in the dark of a bar, my drunk friend while her boyfriend was in the bathroom, a tall boy with a ponytail I didn't know, the male friend who was in love with my roommate. Anyone I could get my hands on was fine with me, as long as I fell asleep pulsing with enough sex to feel immortal or so drunk that I was unaware I was alive.

A GUIDE TO PASSING

"You know, Erin, I don't think you're a lesbian."

My friend Suzanne is an attractive dark-skinned Texan whose opinion of me I value, but to this, I don't know what to say. "Why?"

"Well, I've known some lesbians, and you're not like them. They were..." she fumbled for words, "I don't know, just not like you."

I've learned to pick up on enough subtle hints and key words to know that what she means is: I'm not fat, short-haired, and manly.

"I mean, if I'm not attracted to men, doesn't that make me a lesbian?"

She looks concerned. "I guess so, but...you're too pretty to be a lesbian."

SPEAKING: THE IMPORTANCE OF PUTTING ON A GOOD VOICE

Ponte Vecchio is a street of gold, and as tourist-laden as it might be, you feel like a king walking down it. Every surface shines and glitters at you, and if the street is less populated, like it is in January, it's like a hall of mirrors.

"Oh my god, that's the girl, that's the one I was telling you about." I said. I dragged my roommate around a corner to point at her across the street. She was gorgeous, and I'd noticed her the first day of orientation in my study abroad program in Florence. We had been there two weeks at this point, and I had already raved about this dark-haired butch to all three of my new roommates, and then there she was – right across the street. She was walking with two other girls I recognized as students of our school, the Studio Art Center International, or SACI for short. I thought quickly and crossed the street.

"Hey, you guys go to SACI, right?" I was uncharacteristically peppy.

"Oh, you are in Illustration! Isn't that class great?" Her dumpy friend who sat across from me in my morning class spoke up. I already had a distinct distaste for this girl after she spent half a class period talking about how great the pigeons in Florence were, but for the sake of this auspicious meeting, I faked an interest in her life.

"Oh, sorry, and what's your name?" I offered my hand to the beautiful girl.

"Hey, I'm Sidney." She shook my hand and I disguised my shock at hearing her speak as I vacantly absorbed the third girl's name. Her voice! – it was so – feminine! I was appalled and concerned. She had short, dark curls and big, unlined eyes. Sneakers, a black pea jacket, a white scarf and no bag – could I possibly be wrong?

I ended the conversation abruptly by saying I needed to get back to my roommates and mulled the girl over in my head for days, consumed with doubt and insecurity. Having been single for three years, I was not in a position to lose my gaydar.

A week later, a spot opened in an Animation class I knew she was in, and I showed up the next day. I couldn't find a good way to talk to her after the first class, so I babbled over nonsense while she, completely oblivious to my interest, casually entertained my rambling and politely said goodbye. I walked back to my apartment alone through the cobbled streets, ignoring the catcalls of the merchants and sidestepping the ubiquitous dog shit that framed my walk home. The next class was in three days. I was determined to figure this girl out.

I showed up to the class in mascara and eyeliner. Our strange, twenty-something friendless professor was on my side, apparently, and he paired us together to complete a project. I spent the entire two hours prying information out of her, and, in the silences, questioning her sexuality to myself. I tried and failed to pay attention to her words instead of her voice. Eventually I learned that we lived around the corner from each other, and in this, I saw a glimmer of hope. We walked back together through the dog-shit filled streets and I flirted and wheedled and pried, but she seemed unaware that I was interested at all.

At the corner where we should have parted ways, I made excuses and proposed dinner. We stopped at her apartment, where she invited her roommate to come along. While debating places we might go for dinner, her roommate suggested the falafel shop next door.

"Ooooh, the one with the beautiful Turkish guy?"

Fuck, I thought. I figured I'd spend the next hour and ten euros having dinner with friends. Friends was not what I was trying to make.

I endured watching her flirt with the man behind the counter before the three of us settled into dinner. As a last-ditch attempt to make myself more obvious, I talked about my ex, leaving off the pronoun, and she seemed to finally pick up on it. She stood up to go to the register.

"Hey, do you want a beer?" she asked. "I'll treat." (Translation: I think you may possibly be interested in me and I am trying to determine for sure if this is the case)

"Oh, no, you don't have to pay." (I am absolutely petrified of rejection, please be a lesbian)

"Oh, you sure?" (I guess she is straight after all)

"Yeah, don't worry." (What the hell else can I say at this point?)

After dinner, we decided to go to a club suggested by the Turkish man. In my element once again, I cornered her against the dark wall. The music might be throbbing Eurotechno instead of familiar Top 40 mashups, but the movements were the same as always. I took her home that night, and every night the following week.

It took over a year for her voice to grow on me. I think it happened when we bought a strap-on and I found out that talking like a girl also means you moan like a girl.

MANHANDLING

At the time I flew from Florence's Amerigo Vespucci Airport to Katowice, I had been dating a girl for about a month. It was the first time I'd ever had a serious, butterfly-inducing crush on someone that was realized, and it was fantastic. She had gone to Rome with her parents for spring break, and I had booked tickets months before to go to Krakow to visit a friend who was studying abroad there. He happened to be a friend I'd made out with a few times before, but that was when we were both drunk and depressed, so neither I nor the girlfriend was worried about anything happening.

My first night there, my friend Peter and his friends took me on a drunken stumbling-tour of Krakow, which I vaguely remember as being inhumanly cold in early March and much taller, wider, and greyer than Florence. That night the two of us walked back to his studio apartment, where sleeping arrangements were decided to be together on his carpeted floor.

Who started what I can't say, but that night, and nearly every night after of my five-day stay in Krakow, I kissed Peter hard in his dark loft. He stripped off my shirt and I undid his pants. I had the same confused thoughts I always do when making out with men – am I supposed to put my hands here? Do they like it if I do this? Why isn't he making any noise? He was hard and strangely dry in my hands, not unpleasant but unfamiliar.

I enjoyed the heat of it, the blur and the exoticness, but I knew I was seriously pushing the limits of the privileges of my open relationship. He absolutely was not going to put anything inside me, that much I was sure of, but I contemplated the idea of a giving him a blowjob. It didn't interest me aesthetically or emotionally, but I had an intellectual desire to find out what might happen and see if it gave me a good story for later – the same reason I sometimes made conversation with homeless men on the bus. The thought of my girlfriend's reaction to this news was enough to make me drop the idea, however.

The last night I was there I, as usual, stopped our heavy breathing moments before anything below the belt started happening.

"No, I can't do this," I said. He sighed, exasperated.

"Well, you're not being a good girlfriend or a good hook-up, so you might as well."

I actually thought he was making a pretty good point, and I told him so, but still, I wasn't going to have sex with him.

We don't have to have sex!" he whined. I rolled my eyes and started to put my pajama shirt back on.

"Oh really? What exactly are we gonna do, then?" I asked. He leaned his head back against the wall, defeated.

"You looked better before you put your shirt on."

I crawled on top of him, one leg on either side of his body, and slapped him hard across the face, and we both laughed about it and fell asleep, his arm around me.

EXPLAINING YOURSELF

"So, like, how do you do it?"

It was a question I'd gotten used to answering by the time I finished high school. As soon as anyone finds out you're a lesbian they try to wheedle their way into the all-important and apparently revelatory question, "But how do you have sex?" The first time I heard it was from a friend in high school, and I had no idea how to answer.

"Um, well...I don't know. However you want to?"

My friend looked at me as if I was perhaps not intelligent enough to understand her question, and repeated it.

"Yeah, but, like...how?"

I was sixteen at the time, and I had no idea yet how frequently I would be asked this question, so I tried to answer honestly.

"Well, I guess the same stuff you would do with a guy, mostly."

She thought it over. "But you're, like, missing something important. It's like, you can do the same stuff you do with a guy, but then there are all these other things you can't do."

After being asked this a few more times in high school, I came up with a metaphor:

"Well, you know how sometimes subs come loaded with peppers and olives and mayonnaise and all this other stuff? But maybe you just don't like all that stuff. Maybe you just want turkey, cheese, and lettuce, and maybe some oil, but that's it. So when you get that extra stuff, it actually makes the sub worse, not better."

When I got to college, I decided I needed a new way to answer the question, but I struggled for something intelligent. Eventually I just got frustrated.

"So Erin, how *do* lesbians have sex?"

"However they fucking want."

ELAINE SEXTON

Cantilever Love

This plank, walk, observation
deck of the great Minneapolis
high-rise theatre
reaches out
to the Mississippi
and Saint Paul,

Pillsbury's smokestacks,
so close they are
almost touchable,
the mother/structure,
left behind, sturdy,

weight-bearing,
safe. We stand, suspended,
midair, on metal/cement,
cantilevered. So much depends
on what we can't touch.

I reach my face
over the edge, past
glass barriers. Spray
from the great river reaches back.
We almost touch. Tender.

Architectural.
I've come here in splints,
jerry-rigged,
insupportable.
It's touching the way

the body keeps
trying, the body
built to house the brain,
the brain built to house the senses,
the senses themselves,

containment facilities,
at once, restless and
content to flare up,
die out. Some,
in cantilever moods,

step out. The sun
fixes itself on the skin
which, in turn, contracts
the way the optic
nerve does. In the dark

white jasmine
opens, and exhales.
Hairs in the nose,
tiny cantilevered planks,
reach out to carry

the scent
back to the brain.
My tongue, cantilevered
from my mouth,
touches the fine down

on the nape of your neck
and lifts
not exactly a flavor
but an idea,
suspended, blindfolded, balanced.

JAN FREEMAN

January

If the back, wide as the field, long as the field
could be touched by the hands, two leaves
two stones, unaccustomed to touch —
would the hands, thin, touch the back
wide as the birch, long as the fallen branch,
hands accustomed to the texture of fabrics, wood,
dexterous, accustomed to sewing and repair;
would the mouths touch, sad mouths
heavy with speech, able to create and remove
salt on surfaces and heat.
Will the legs, completely different dimensions
twist like rope or become bridges,
bring the bodies closer through the variations
of hum and moisture.
Break, now break again; close the eyes and sleep before
any part of the potential collision begins.
The neck, the hair, the skin —
can they meet before the minds
waken or could the mouths waken, leading the rest
to a slow spinning,
as the frown can be slow
living for years beneath the smile,
loyal, holding the smile back,
master of interference
when texture might be one afternoon
of rising temperature midwinter
as the snow turns to corn-snow,
and the skin pushes the frown out like a splinter
focused pressure
or the hands which might cleanse the back, the neck,

the breasts through touch,
the bodies pliable as snow in the day's melt
before the temperature rises higher and then
drops again,
changed through a conflagration of the senses
before the redwings fly, long before
the robins fly, and the fields reveal themselves
as extensions of the bodies who hold
their bird hearts inside lead boxes
inhibiting movement, the edges cutting,
bruising the parts of the body that skin cannot reach
but words can reach, intangible, moving like the beech leaves move
when the months are frozen without thought or emotion.

Pomegranate

As my lover bloodies the countertop,
I think of Persephone's mother
who made winter – six seeds.
Six months in the hospital
when I was princess of the black chamber too.
My mother's ear pressed to the plateau of my back
listening to the wheeze,
pleading my pulmonary self to re-awaken,
to climb out of the diaphragmed dark
kicking muscles between each rung of my ribcage
so they might be spurred into contraction,
that slow drawing in and release I re-learned
to breathe spring. My lover uses her fingers
to scoop swollen arils, hollowing a cavity in the lobes.
She presses her cheek to my breast, says *you're wheezing*.
But my lungs are only making the noise of translation,
sputtering through languages so both understand:
the pneuma in my chest has grown into a river.
It has filled pools in the courtyards of both worlds
and waits now at the ferry, even as they eavesdrop
faces pressed to my back and front banks.

ERIC SASSON

Body and Mind

IT FASCINATES HIM, all the things he can do without ever getting up from the bed: turn off the lights. Close the blinds and the curtains. Set an alarm, check voicemail, order room service, switch from TV to DVD to WebTV. He can even phone in Keno numbers and charge them to the room.

Andy spreads himself out, foraging through a bag of Cheez Doodles. He's adjusted the thermostat twice and yet the air in the room remains bone chilling. It's his first time in Sin City. Hunter comes to Vegas several times a year on business, and when the Wynn sent him a comp for four free nights, he parlayed it into an early anniversary present.

On the TV: Notes on a Scandal. Young Steven Connolly is coming on to Sheba Hart, played by Cate Blanchett. He keeps calling her 'Miss'. Andy and Hunter have seen the film several times. They bonded over the campy drama during their first month of dating. Of course she'd risk her marriage. Look at him! Andy said. So he's sixteen, Hunter said. He's worth some jail time. Andy's eyes narrowed impishly. Later that night they fucked like wind-up toys whose bezels had been turned to snapping.

His phone buzzes: both he and Hunter are on Grindr, and Bigg-Rigg9x10 has sent him an opening "hey." BiggRigg's picture has a face, which is a plus, but his stats say forty-three, outside of Hunter's age range. Hunter is seven years older and still maintains a stricter cutoff than Andy does. Andy sometimes wonders what will happen when he gets to that cutoff date, if Hunter will trade him in for a newer model.

The bathroom door opens, and he catches a glimpse of Hunter's hairy thigh in the hallway mirror.

"Sorry." Hunter sounds defensive. "The WiFi doesn't work when it's closed."

So now he's priggish just because he doesn't want to see his boyfriend taking a dump. "BiggRigg said hello to me," he says.

"Is he sexy?" Hunter asks.

"I think so." Andy grabs the remote to turn up the volume. Judi Dench has just been introduced to Cate Blanchett's much older husband and Down-syndrome son. The narrative voice-over is deliciously cruel.

"He's old," Hunter says, dismissively.

You're old, Andy thinks. "I like older guys," he says, instead.

"I know," Hunter says. "Let's keep looking."

They're about to celebrate four years together. Andy got his iPhone several months after Hunter did. Now we can window-shop together, he joked that night. Hunter grimaced, but the comment wasn't meant to be cutting. And Hunter was the one who brought it up a few weeks before their trip: Should we go on Grindr in Vegas? It was a sensitive topic, considering Andy's infidelity the year before. Hunter was being mature about it, all things considered. They'd recently started talking about three ways again, vaguely, like one talks about adoption or moving to a new city. Andy wanted to believe the suggestion meant Hunter was moving on, so he smiled, and paused—a bit theatrically—before he took Hunter's hand and said sure, why not.

An ad for Absolut pops up on the bottom of the screen. Someone's rich, Andy thinks. By arranging people according to distance, Grindr cuts straight to the chase: Gay men want dick and they don't want to travel, or at least they want the traveling they do to be in proportion with the magnificence of said dick. Then again, he and Hunter met on a chat site. So you dig Asians? he'd asked Hunter, early on in their first chat. He had to, since it wasn't unusual on these sites to find white men writing nasty tercets like "No fats, femmes or Asians." Turned out Hunter had dated several Filipinos.

He sends out two hellos: to Homotextual, to IMNneedofcock, both younger than him, yet more manly than Hunter usually likes.

Are you alone? Homotextual writes back. Andy smirks; both he and Hunter put "Couple looking for 3rd" as their status line.

I'm with my boyfriend, he writes. He's on too. NYCBeast. Where r u?

@ a bar off Harmony, Homotextual writes back. And then, a minute later, after presumably checking out Hunter's photo: I can be there in 10.

Andy wonders about being online while in a bar, if one doesn't defeat the purpose of the other. Then again, it's just after 2am, and the options at the bar are likely whittling down to troll territory. "What about Homotextual?" he calls out.

"I'll check," Hunter says.

"He wants to come over," Andy says, flipping through the stations. Who's Afraid of Virginia Woolf is on AMC. It's a hard call; Elizabeth Taylor has great lines. But Judi Dench is about to fondle Cate Blanchett's hands. He switches back to Notes.

"Hold on."

Andy hears an odd tapping coming from the bathroom. Hunter is limping. Andy guesses his leg must have fallen asleep from sitting too long on the toilet. He laughs, then sighs, as Hunter fumbles with his pants.

Sex with Hunter used to be great. Hot. Smoking hot. Raw. Three, four times a day. Moments when time stopped. Moments when he felt like he was part of one grand, pulsating engine of lust. Belts. Handcuffs. Dildos and I'm gonna breed you, you dirty fucking cumrag.

They crossed lines. He liked it when they crossed lines, when Hunter smacked him, spit on him, said obscene things, things that shouldn't be said outside of a bedroom.

And then it slowed. Not all of a sudden. The flood became a river, then a stream, then a trickle. Sex became stale. Worse, a chore, like laundry, like clipping toenails. He worried for a while. Hunter was losing interest, Hunter no longer found him attractive. But it wasn't that simple. He didn't initiate either; it was more of a mutual decision.

The lack of passion left him feeling disconnected, undesirable. When he hooked up that first time, he hoped to get these thoughts out of his system. A few others followed, all random guys he found online. Shortly after, Andy confessed, hoping to spark some dialogue. Which it did. Healthy dialogue. Meaningful dialogue. Hunter said: I understand. Hunter said: We'll work through this. And they did; the sex not only resumed, it got hotter. Nastier, as if Hunter had something to prove. Andy wasn't about to complain. The sizzle was back. A brief, beautiful burst. And then.

"Let's pass on Homotextual," Hunter says. He comes out of the bathroom, sits down on the opposite bed. Andy types his regrets and they share a quick, flat smile of acknowledgment. Hunter, still so lovely to look at. Rugged and masculine, a man one pictures in flannel.

It's not like they've stopped getting along. If anything, the affection between them has grown. They're like lesbians now, experiencing the inevitable bed death. Why did affection have to be the death knell of lust? What is it about hugging Hunter that makes Andy's dick limp? Or rather, not limp, but awake for the briefest spell, like a bear that peeks out of his cave only to decide his winter isn't over. He told his friend Kevin about it one night over too many drinks, and Kevin said: Maybe you shouldn't be together then. Andy laughed. Single people always thought they saw things more clearly.

"Hey," Hunter says. "Check out Sexxyboi26."

Andy watches Hunter's face, the way his eyebrows raise and his lips turn inside his mouth. There's something forced and hollow about this expression. Hunter types furiously into his phone, and then he laughs: short, sharp tremors of breath. It unnerves Andy, this laugh. He hates the familiarity of it, the freedom of it. So Sexxyboi is interesting, so he's prince fucking charming. He doesn't get why Hunter shot down Homotextual, who's clearly hot enough. No doubt it has something to do with that laugh.

Then he checks. In the photo Sexxyboi wears a baseball cap and jeans. He's shirtless and thin, white, mostly smooth, aside from the treasure trail leading down to his boxer briefs, poking out from underneath. He has a tattoo of a leprechaun on his right arm. His eyes are gray and his lips chewy, like fresh taffy. His expression isn't just vacant, but suggestive of a deep, piercing emptiness, the kind of look fashion photographers solicit from models on billboards advertising fragrances. Sexy, like a Popsicle can be sexy: refreshingly sexy. The kind of guy who hand-washes his car, who holds the hose between his legs and lets the water soak his t-shirt.

"Looks great." Andy smiles, eagerly. He thinks Hunter wants him eager.

"He's in the lobby," Hunter says.

"Invite him up," Andy says.

Hunter stares back. "You sure?"

"What do you mean? Should I not be?"

"Of course not," Hunter says. "I'm feeling this'll be a good thing."

"Are you going to fuck him?" Andy says. "I want you to fuck him."

"Ok," Hunter says. He looks down at the floor. "Do you want him to fuck you?"

"I don't know," Andy says. "Do you want him to?"

"Do I look fatter to you?" Hunter gets up and stands by the full-length mirror, needlessly sucking in his gut.

"You look sexy," Andy says.

Hunter sighs and stares at himself. Andy takes two bottles of Vodka from the mini-bar and puts them on the desk. He rinses his ass in the sink and dabs some cologne on the back of his neck while Hunter throws dirty clothes into their luggage, straightens the towels, finds the lube in his toiletry bag and slips it into the nightstand drawer. They feed each other breath strips.

They stand, face to face. Hunter takes a deep breath. Andy does too, and Hunter's eyes widen. They're nervous; it's normal to be nervous. He wants to say something before Sexxyboi gets there. Maybe not say something, but do something: a gesture, an affirmation of his love. Four years. Andy thinks back to moving day. Suddenly Hunter was always there. Suddenly he'd turn around and Hunter was adding vitamins to the pantry, creams to the medicine cabinet. Was this alright with him? It was frightening, and then it wasn't It was ordinary.

There's a rapping at the door. Andy watches Hunter fix his hair one last time in the mirror. Hunter's fingers fumble on the doorknob. He straightens his back and just as he takes another long breath, Andy wonders if he should stop him. He didn't think Hunter would be this anxious. He wonders where he should his place himself: Standing by the window? Sitting on a chair, the bed? No, not the bed.

I can't tell you not to have sex with someone else, he'd told Hunter that night, months after his confession. I just want us to be emotionally monogamous. Hunter nodded repeatedly. Of course, he said, as if picking up on a subtext Andy wasn't sure he was implying. It hadn't been a suggestion, or a license, or a warning; Andy just wanted them to be realistic. He has little empathy for the women on daytime TV talk shows, crying about their cheating partners. Don't they get it? Men like variety. It doesn't matter if you're the juiciest steak in the world; even unrepentant meat-eaters want a pizza now and again. He loves Hunter, and he still fucked around. And who knows, maybe Hunter fucked around too. With someone younger or someone with a thicker cock or even someone who just smelled different. It didn't matter, so long as the love between them stayed strong.

Hunter opens the door. Sexxyboi leans against the frame, one hand behind the trucker cap on his head. He's taller than Andy pictured him to be, taller and bonier. Still, sexy; ridiculously sexy. He doesn't respond when Hunter offers his hand, not right away. Instead he looks past Hunter to Andy, his mouth opening to a squiggly, mischievous smile.

"Marcel," he says, finally shaking Hunter's hand.

The tension in Hunter's face snaps into relief, and Andy realizes that what seemed like anxiety before was more likely enthusiasm. Hunter introduces himself, then Andy, who waves from his seat by the desk, not yet willing to get up. But Marcel makes the move anyway.

"Pleasure to meet you." Marcel shakes Andy's hand with both of his own. "So you boys are from New York? I've lived there."

"Whereabouts?" Andy asks.

"Here and there," Marcel says. He puts his hands on his hips and eyes Hunter quizzically. "You seem familiar. Have we met before?"

Hunter's eyebrows arch. He clears his throat. "I don't think so."

Andy gauges Hunter's expression, the quiet surprise in it. He thinks of stoplights, how red lights seem stern and serious, and green lights almost seem to be smiling at you. Hunter's face is a yellow light, he thinks, not sure whether to slow down or hurry up.

"Can I fix you something?" Andy heads for the vodka.

"I'm good," Marcel says. He looks at Hunter and sighs. His eyes canvass the room, and then lock on Andy's; it's a pushy, puzzled look, like he's trying to determine Andy's place in the universe. Andy wonders if Marcel is on something, a mood stabilizer or enhancer.

"Take a seat," Hunter says.

Marcel heads to the bed. "You guys play together often?"

Hunter and Andy turn to each other. "Sometimes," Andy says.

"Sometimes," Marcel repeats. "It's good to spice things up."

"Yeah," Hunter says, forcing a grin.

"That's why I'm here." Marcel claps his hands. "To spice things up."

"We're glad," Andy says. The TV is still on. Andy grabs the remote, considers turning it off, and instead, lowers the volume. Judi Dench is promising to protect Cate from harm.

"So you're an Oriental," Marcel says, nodding at Andy. He reclines on the bed with one hand twisted behind his back, the other lifting up the front of his t-shirt. The word, followed quickly by the offered peek of Marcel's abs, unsettles Andy. He takes both in and lets them simmer.

Hunter laughs, tensely. "He's not a rug."

Marcel shakes his head. "Well I can see that. He's as smooth as they come."

"I'm Filipino," Andy says. He sits down beside Marcel, the vacuous stare from the photo somehow more menacing in person. He wonders if Marcel's comment is meant to trouble him, excite him, or both. He's not sure why exactly, but the cloudier his thoughts get the more his body longs to find out what's next. He takes Marcel's hand into his lap and starts drawing circles up the man's sinewy forearm and taut bicep. Marcel doesn't resist.

"No one says Oriental anymore." Hunter's voice is slow and low. He studies Andy's expression, searching for an accomplice to his offense. But I'm not offended, Andy thinks.

"I'm confused," Marcel says, looking first at Andy, then at Hunter. "The Philippines are in Asia, right? Where are Filipinos from?"

Andy laughs; Marcel isn't confused. Andy looks at Hunter, nods at the empty space on the other side of the bed. "Sit down, Hunter," he says.

Hunter doesn't move. Andy lifts Marcel's shirt higher, revealing sleek muscles and creamy nipples, dusted with a few tufts of gossamer hair. Andy is aroused. He knows Hunter must be too.

"Oriental refers to objects from Asia." Hunter shakes his head. The words sound labored, schoolmarmish. "People are Asian."

Marcel smiles at Andy, revealing dimples. Dimples which make him look naive or stupid, Andy isn't sure which. He takes Andy's hand and puts it on his belt buckle. "So are you Asian? Is that where you're from, Pumpkin?"

Hunter walks behind Andy. He reaches over and takes his boyfriend's hand off of Marcel and squeezes Andy's shoulders, firmly, protectively. Andy looks up, irritated. It's not like Hunter to get worked up over silly comments. It's not like him to refuse to take a joke.

"He's from Queens," Hunter says.

"Filipinos are from Queens?" Marcel asks.

Andy chuckles. Marcel's being an ass. Marcel pokes him playfully in the stomach and laughs too. Still, Andy is certain they're not laughing at the same thing.

Andy shoots Hunter a placating look. "Relax," he says.

"I think my Uncle is Filipino," Marcel says. "He's a rabbi in Forest Hills."

Andy reaches for Hunter's hand, which is wet and tight. He wants to ease his boyfriend back into the moment. What does it matter what Marcel says? Hunter's jaw is clenched. He's tapping his loose hand against his thigh. He's angry, and Marcel isn't picking up on the cues—or maybe he is. Maybe Marcel wants Hunter angry. Maybe Marcel wants Hunter to fuck the anger into him.

"Wait, he's Ashkenazi, though," Marcel says. "Wouldn't Filipinos be Sephardic? Because of Spanish Ancestry? I feel so dumb."

Marcel bites his index finger. His eyes are too big for his face, innocent, dewy eyes that remind Andy of cartoon deer. But Marcel isn't innocent. Marcel has a swagger. Marcel lounges on their bed without being invited. He takes what he wants, says what he wants, in the manner of a gambler who's grown used to winning. Marcel knows what he's doing, Andy thinks. Let him call me Oriental. I want to be Oriental tonight.

"I wouldn't know." Andy puts his hand back on Marcel's crotch, looks up at Hunter and sighs a 'let's-get-on-with-this' sigh. "I'm not Jewish."

Hunter's eyes tilt to Andy, then retreat. "He's not 'from' Asia. He wasn't born in the Philippines so it's not accurate so say he's 'from' there. He's from Queens," he says.

"This isn't necessary," Andy says. He looks at Marcel, whose smirk is more jovial than angry. Andy studies the smirk. He thinks he understands now: Marcel is playing a game, and Hunter is the prize. Marcel is jealous; he wonders how a man they just met could already be jealous.

"Right. So he's Oriental and from Queens," Marcel says. "I get it now."

"Your use of the word Oriental is just plain stupid at this point,"

Hunter says. He cups his forehead with his right hand and rubs his temples. Andy wishes he was moved. He wants to be touched by the gallantry, the sensitivity on Hunter's part, but he isn't. Because Marcel is playing. And since Hunter has to know that, then maybe Hunter's playing too.

"Take off my shoes," Marcel says. He's staring at Hunter, but Andy knows he's the one being addressed. He doesn't need to be asked twice. He slides down the bed, and lifts Marcel's right leg in the air, languidly slipping the man's loafer off of his foot. Marcel's sock is damp at the heel and toes. The soft, buttery scent of sweat fills the air. Andy shoves his face into the man's foot and inhales. He opens his eyes and looks at Hunter as he sucks on Marcel's toes. Hunter stands rigid, frozen in place. He looks like a wounded dog. No, not a dog, a wolf, a wounded wolf staring into the eyes of the giraffe it tried to attack and which had kicked it, hard.

"Let me ask you, Hunter," Marcel says. He seems indifferent to Andy's kink, indifferent as a Queen to the vassals performing her daily pedicure. Instead he makes for Hunter's thigh, just within reach of his left hand. "Is Oriental only Chinese, Japanese and Korean?"

"The term Oriental is offensive to Asians." Hunter's voice is quavering. Still Andy ignores him. He decides to brave Marcel's other foot. He takes a sidelong glance, sees that Hunter is hard, sees that he wishes he wasn't.

"All the Orientals I know don't seem to mind," Marcel says. "But then again, they're from Asia, not Queens."

"They do mind. They just don't tell you. Ask them."

Marcel laughs. "I don't speak Oriental though."

"No need to continue this." Hunter walks towards the door. "You should leave."

"Should I?" Marcel says. "Really? You want me to leave?"

"No," Andy says. "Please stay, Mister. Me so horny. Me love you long time!"

Marcel laughs. Hunter turns white as an envelope. "Jesus Christ, Andy," he says.

"He wants me to stay," Marcel says, a meaty vein in his neck pulsating as he stares at Hunter. "Do you want me to stay?"

"This isn't going to work," Hunter says, throwing up his hands.

"Why not?" Andy asks. Hunter is getting furious. And now he's going to call it off because of what, their dignity? Andy doesn't need someone protecting his dignity. He thinks about Hunter's laugh earlier, the look on his face when Marcel walked in. This strange look of disorientation, but also of regret, like Hunter had forgotten the events of a magical day and seeing Marcel had reminded him, brought back this rush of memories.

"Andy, can I please talk to you alone?" Hunter says.

Andy doesn't move. He can't remember the last time he was this turned on. He sees that Hunter is turned on despite himself and he imagines Marcel is turning himself on too. They're on the threshold of one spectacular fuck, one mind-blowing fuck that will sear into their memory and erase months of bad sex, and he could turn around, he could waver and negotiate with Hunter, but he senses, deeply, that this is not what Hunter wants, to pseudo-save him from this asshole who may be a real asshole but who was more likely just playing one.

Instead he unbuckles Marcel's belt. He rips open the button fly, tugs Marcel's pants off of his legs and pulls on the elastic band of his boxers. Marcel is large, punishingly hard. And yet quivering, almost shy, now that he's naked.

"Are you happy?" Marcel looks up at Hunter with eerie surprise, his smirk practically hostile. "Are you getting what you want?"

And then Andy knows.

He's not sure exactly how he knows, if it's the catastrophic chill in Hunter's eyes, directed at Marcel, or the spastic flaring of his nostrils. Or is it Marcel that tells him everything, Marcel whose deer eyes are suddenly not so cartoonish after all. Andy proceeds to deep throat him; he watches Marcel's mouth droop in shock, his eyes clouding, not with pleasure, not exactly shame. Andy stares into those eyes as his head bobs back and forth, and thinks of the white sheets artists place over their canvasses, to delay the moment of surprise. Marcel's eyes are a white sheet and Hunter and his dithering another white sheet and Andy has lifted too soon; the work wasn't ready, apparently. They needed more time.

And once he knows, he can't stop. He won't stop. He's going to oblige, perform his part spectacularly. He gets up from the bed, strips down naked before them. He sees his reflection in the mirror beside the television, his soft, smooth, brown skin, his small nipples, his frail arms. Not a man's body. A boy's body. A body meant to submit.

"Andy, please," Hunter says.

Andy shushes him. "Get undressed, Hunter."

He asks Hunter to pass him a condom. When he insists, Hunter doesn't refuse. Andy reaches for the lube from the nightstand, squirts a few drops and massages it into his hands. He lubricates himself from behind and throws the condom onto Marcel's stomach. Marcel stares at the packet, and looks across at Hunter. Hunter nods and Marcel opens it, quickly ripping the foil with his teeth. He slides it over his cock.

Andy straddles him. The heavy murmur of their breaths is interrupted by the murderous screams from the TV, audible despite the low volume: Cate Blanchett is finally tearing into Judi Dench, finally accusing her of all that's coming to her. He rides Marcel and thinks of how long it's been since he's ridden Hunter. He thinks of Stephen Connelly, and his devilish chivalry, his infernal magnetism and how tough it is, even after several anniversaries, for someone to resist the cruelty of beauty.

He rides. Marcel is pounding back, unforgiving. Andy closes his eyes and imagines floods and fires, supernovas fading, dying beautifully. When he opens them Hunter has taken off his pants. He masturbates right by Marcel's face, slapping his cock against Marcel's cheeks in a way that makes Andy laugh whenever Hunter does it to him, a laugh which Andy knows irritates Hunter. He wonders if Hunter is as happy as he is now. He wonders if he's making Hunter happy, finally. He wants to see beyond Hunter's façade and make the inside of Hunter happy, the part that must hate him. That part that will not forgive.

But there's no point in thinking of happiness, or forgiveness. There's no point in understanding, because now there is only this moment, this final act, this searing, mind-bending, scorching and insanely pleasurable moment, hotter than ever before, absurdly hot, inhumanly hot. They switch positions, everyone fucks, everyone is fucked, and when Andy asks both of them to penetrate him at the same time, they do. And when he asks Marcel and Hunter to call him a chink, a gook, a dog-eating faggot, they supply even more adjectives; they coin new phrases. They can't settle for less now, this is the only way it can be.

Once everyone is spent, Andy lies between Hunter and Marcel, who have both turned away from him to face opposite walls. He stares up at the ceiling and listens to the thrum of their breaths, feeling the weight of the silence. Soon they all shift; it's not possible to remain on a bed after a moment like this, not possible to bask in a pleasure so brittle and fleeting. Marcel heads to the bathroom. Hunter searches for the remote; Notes on A Scandal is long over. Now it's Sleepless in Seattle. Hunter and Andy hate Sleepless in Seattle. Andy sits up and stares into Hunter's eyes. He stares hard, like staring might provide insight, like staring might express his feelings.

He thinks back to the first time they had sex after his confession. Hunter had entered him raw, right on the living room floor, and when he yelped, Hunter had covered his mouth, told him to shut up and take it. He doesn't know why these images consume him. Perhaps Hunter understands this better than he does. Perhaps he really has provided the perfect anniversary present. These thoughts echo in his brain, even above the din of his anger and disgust.

When Marcel comes out of the bathroom he slips into his jeans and shirt and adjusts his hat. "That was quite an adventure, boys," he says.

Hunter looks away and Andy attempts a smile. Neither says a word.

"I'd like to say I wish you both the best." Marcel claps his hands.

"But I don't." His eyes fixate on Hunter. His lips tremble then open to release a croaking, jittery laugh. "You're perfect for each other," he says, no longer attempting to disguise his sarcasm. He tips his hat and heads out the door.

Hunter gets up. He grabs the Cheez Doodles and shoves a few into his mouth before resealing the bag and putting it on the dresser. He washes the mess down with some vodka.

"Sit down," Andy says.

But Hunter doesn't. He paces the room, rearranging tourist brochures on the desk. Andy knows conversation won't settle him. But conversation isn't optional now.

"Please sit down," Andy says, and this time Hunter stops, and sits, on the far side of the bed.

"How long have you been seeing him?" Andy asks. He slides closer, reaches for Hunter's hand. He's the one who should need comforting, but instead, this: Hunter on the verge of tears. Hunter about to collapse into a ball of yarn, unraveling, unraveling. It's Hunter's world that's been shattered.

"I didn't think he'd be so cruel," Hunter says. He pulls down on the lids of his eyes, his defeat complete.

"Do you love him?" Andy asks.

Hunter's lips tremble. "I love you," he says. But Andy is unmoved. It sounds more like a justification than a statement.

"Yes," Andy says. That wasn't the question, he thinks.

"I won't see him again," Hunter says.

"I think he loves you," Andy says. "Despite everything."

"I don't give a shit!" Hunter's face is a blubbery mess. Andy wonders whether he should cry too. He wonders if he can. "How could you... why did you let him say those things to you?"

Andy sighs. Was Hunter serious? "You say those things to me. You call me bitch, humiliate me. I wanted you to do those things to me."

"It's not the same."

"No," Andy says. "Maybe not."

"So what, are you leaving me now?" Hunter asks.

"If you did this," Andy says. "Haven't you already left?"

"You left first." Hunter grinds his teeth, his face darkening, his eyes penetrating and sober. "You cheated first."

"I know." Andy tries to hold Hunter's gaze. "You said you forgave me. And since then, I've asked for one thing."

"But you can't ask. You don't get to ask." Hunter stands up. He grabs the remote from the bed and throws it across the room. Andy watches the batteries spill out and bounce on the carpet. He follows Hunter's pace with his eyes, wanting to understand his anger, wondering if he should share in it, or just accommodate it. But it's too brief: in a few seconds Hunter is sitting beside him. He cups Andy's cheeks, his eyes feral and desperate. "Listen, I don't love him. I swear to God I don't."

He pushes Hunter away. "I asked for one thing."

"I know." Hunter begins to whimper. "I'm sorry. But it was good, wasn't it? It was really good."

"It's over," Andy says. He turns away, walks into the bathroom. He's still naked. Hunter's phone rests on the vanity. He picks it up, opens Grindr, notices several messages pending. He sighs, puts the phone down and stares at himself in the mirror, at the vessel containing him. A needy vessel. Greedy and possessive.

He wonders if he'll really leave Hunter. He wonders if, in a few hours from now, while he's asleep, Hunter will stir him awake, and beg him for forgiveness. And when he refuses, when he insists that he hates Hunter and wishes him dead, perhaps then Hunter will stop crying and begging. Perhaps Hunter will stop listening and take him by force, and then, suddenly, the lust will return to haunt them again, that fierce, primordial lust, that all-consuming fire which will scorch them, swallow them, remind them that they are alive.

LISA ALEXANDER is working towards her MFA in poetry at Drew University, and is a member of The Madwomen in the Attic writing workshop. Her work has appeared in journals such as *The Burnside Review, The Palimpsest Review*, and anthologized in *Voices from the Attic*. She's a sound engineer for *Prosody*, NPR-affiliate WESA's weekly show featuring the work of National writers. Among her favorite poets are May Swenson and Frank O'Hara. She likes all blue flowers.

NICKOLE BROWN's debut, *Sister*, a novel-in-poems, was published by Red Hen Press. "A Book of Birds," a key poem from her forthcoming collection of poetry won AROHO's Orlando Poetry Prize in 2010. She graduated from The Vermont College of Fine Arts and was the editorial assistant for the late Hunter S. Thompson. She has received grants from the National Endowment for the Arts, the Kentucky Foundation for Women, and the Kentucky Arts Council. She worked at Sarabande Books for ten years. Currently, she is the Editor for the Marie Alexander Series in Prose Poetry and works as the National

Publicity Consultant for Arktoi Books, an imprint dedicated to publishing one book by a lesbian author annually. She lives in Little Rock, AR, where she is the Assistant Professor poetry at University of Arkansas. She's reading Carol Guess' new book of lyrical essays, *My Father in Water*, and she still thinks Liz Bradfield's *Interpretive Work* is one of the best poetry collections around. Her favorite flower is the peony, fleshsoft and pink and frantic with ants.

AUSTIN BUNN is a writer, playwright and performer. His work has appeared in *The Atlantic Monthly, Zoetrope, The New York Times Magazine, One Story, The Pushcart Prize* anthology and elsewhere. Favorite LGBT authors? Andrew Holleran (*Grief* is on the nightstand), Adam Haslett (utterly convinced me about inner life), Alan Hollinghurst (can filigree a sentence like no other), Ed White (the ultimate stylist), Paul Monette (I had his dorm room!), and Pinups (which is not an author but very much belongs here). Favorite flower? Whatever's in the clearance aisle at Fruitbasket Flowerland.

BRENT CALDERWOOD's poems have appeared in *Crab Creek Review, The Gay & Lesbian Review Worldwide, Gertrude, Poets & Artists, American Poetry Journal*, and *The Southern Poetry Anthology*. He is the Literary Editor for *A&U* magazine and an Associate Editor at *Assaracus* and LambdaLiterary.org. His favorite LGBT writers include James Baldwin, Ellen Bass, Mark Doty, and Langston Hughes. His favorite flower is the California golden poppy.

Originally from Milwaukee, Wisconsin, **MONICA CARTER** currently resides in Los Angeles, California where she is a current participant in PEN Center USA's Mark program for Emerging Voices alumni. A PEN USA Emerging Voices Fellow 2010 and a Lambda Literary Foundation Emerging GLBT Voice 2010, her fiction has appeared in *Strange Cargo, An Emerging Voices Anthology, Black Clock 12*, and *The Rattling Wall*. The writers she admires are Edmund White, Emma

Donoghue and Jane Bowles. Her favorite flowers are the kind given to her.

CHERYL DUMESNIL's first collection of poems, *In Praise of Falling*, won the 2008 Agnes Lynch Starrett Prize. She edited *Hitched! Wedding Stories from San Francisco City Hall* and co-edited, with Kim Addonizio, *Dorothy Parker's Elbow: Tattoos on Writers, Writers on Tattoos*. As a regular correspondent on www.outandaround.com, Dumesnil reports from the crossroads of parenthood, suburbia, and lesbian life. Currently reading: Steve Fellner's *The Weary World Rejoices*. Favorite flower: the passion flower growing on the chain link fence near 6th and Irving in San Francisco.

JIM ELLEDGE's *H*, a collection of prose poems about artist Henry Darger, is due April 2012 from Lethe Press. Also forthcoming are *Who's Yer Daddy? Gay Writers Celebrate Their Mentors and Forerunners*, co-edited with David Groff (Wisconsin) and *Throw-Away Boy: A Life of Henry Darger* (Overlook). His *A History of My Tattoo* won the 2006 Lambda Literary Award. His favorite flower is the orange blossom of the flamboyant tree. He's come to realize that the work of many poets younger than he—Peter Covino, David Groff, Charles Jensen, Brian Teare—mentor him as much than those he grew to adulthood reading.

GINA R. EVERS earned her MFA in creative writing from American University, where she teaches in the College Writing Program and creates the alumni magazine for the International Legal Studies Program, among other responsibilities. Her poems have appeared or are forthcoming in *Copper Nickel, Assaracus, Shady Side Review*, and *IC View*. Gina was also named one of the Emerging LGBT Voices of 2010 by the Lambda Literary Foundation. She lives in Washington, DC with her soon-to-be wife, and Gina's favorite flower is the hibiscus.

JAN FREEMAN is co-editor of *Sisters: An Anthology*, and author of *Simon Says* (nominated for an NBCC in poetry) and *Hyena* (winner of the CSU poetry center prize). She is director and founder of Paris Press, a not-for-profit publisher of groundbreaking literature by women that has been overlooked by mainstream publishers. "I've been having a lot of fun reading May Swenson. Her love poems and erotica—wild, luscious, funny—and wise. In addition, I've been reading Lorca's *Ode to Walt Whitman*, Alice B. Toklas, poems by Jeff Oaks, Liz Ahl, Robin Becker, and about to finally dive into Alison Bechdel's *Fun Home*. And always Whitman, always Rukeyser's poems about the body, her erotica. As the season shifts to winter, I seem to be looking for poems with physical heat — and poems that make me laugh. They balance sadness, illness, loss, and offer space to breathe."

CELESTE GAINEY has had a long career as a lighting designer for both film and architecture. She is a 2010 graduate of Carlow University's MFA program. Her chapbook, *In the land of speculation & seismography*, a runner-up for the 2010 Robin Becker Chapbook Prize was recently published by Seven Kitchens Press in their 2011 Summer Kitchen Series. Her current LGBT reading includes Stacey Waite's *The Lake Has No Saint*, Aaron Smith's *In the Company of Men*, and Jen Benka's *Pinko*. Her favorite flower is the sunflower, but she always brakes for fields of wild California poppies.

THOMAS GLAVE is the author of *Whose Song? and Other Stories*, *The Torturer's Wife* (Lambda Literary Award finalist, 2008), and the essay collection *Words to Our Now: Imagination and Dissent* (Lambda Literary Award, 2005). He is editor of the anthology *Our Caribbean: A Gathering of Lesbian and Gay Writing from the Antilles* (Lambda Literary Award, 2008). He teaches at SUNY Binghamton, and in 2012 will be a Visiting Fellow at Clare Hall, Cambridge University. Favorite flower: Geranium. Favorite LGBT writers: several, but especially Dionne Brand and Jean Genet.

DAPHNE GOTTLIEB stitches together the ivory tower and the gutter just using her tongue. She the is the author and editor of eight award-winning books in at least three genres. There will soon be a ninth with the spring publication of *Dear Dawn: Aileen Wuornos in her own words*, co-edited with Lisa Kester. Her favorite queer authors include David Wojnarovicz, Kathy Acker, William Burroughs, and Aileen Wuornos. She is devotedly a fan of peonies and chocolate cosmos.

JAMES ALLEN HALL is the author of *Now You're the Enemy*, which won the Lambda Literary Award. The recipient of 2011 Fellowships in Poetry from the National Endowment for the Arts and the New York Foundation for the Arts, he teaches creative writing and literature at the State University of New York-Potsdam. He is inspired by the likes of James Baldwin, Paul Monette, Audre Lorde, and Adrienne Rich, among many others. He has recently devoured Manuel Munoz's novel, *What You See in the Dark*, is currently reading Julie Marie Wade's lyric essay collection, *Small Fires*, and is teaching Jericho Brown's book of poems, *Please*. His favorite flower is the torch azalea.

MATTHEW HITTINGER is the author of three chapbooks and the collection *Skin Shift*, forthcoming from Sibling Rivalry Press in 2012. He's currently reading *Dear Prudence: New and Selected Poems* by David Trinidad. His favorite flower is the marigold, and he lives and works in New York City.

ALICIA SHANDRA HOLMES has published fiction in *The Bitter Oleander, Rosebud, CRATE, Many Mountains Moving*, and *The Blue Earth Review*. She most recently was a resident at the Kerouac House of Orlando and the Blue Mountain Center. She lives in Michigan.

A 2011 Pushcart Prize Nominee, **SAEED JONES** received his MFA in Creative Writing at Rutgers University–Newark. His poetry has appeared or is forthcoming in publications like B*lackbird, Hayden's Ferry Review, StorySouth, Jubilat, West Branch* & *The Collagist*. His chapbook *When the Only Light is Fire* is available from Sibling Rivalry Press. His blog is **For Southern Boys Who Consider Poetry**. Favorite flower: Amaryllis. "LGBT writers I admire or are reading right now: Metta Sama, Jericho Brown, D.A. Powell, Audre Lorde."

JOAN LARKIN's most recent book is *My Body: New and Selected Poems* (Hanging Loose). Her chapbook *Legs Tipped with Small Claws* is forthcoming from Argos Books. She is a 2011 recipient of the Shelley Memorial Award and the Academy of American Poets Fellowship. "I'm rereading Mae Swenson — her mastery and quirky vision are a never-ending source of pleasure and surprise. As for flowers: a friend whose passion is growing old roses introduced me to Great Maiden's Blush; when she told me that it's also called Cuisse de Nymphe, I knelt at the suggestion of delicious thigh, inhaled its heady perfume, and swooned."

ABBIE J. LEAVENS was born in Iowa. She now lives in Irvine, California where she studies and writes. She has always enjoyed reading poems by Allen Ginsberg. More recently she has enjoyed the writing of David Sedaris and poems by Gabrielle Calvocoressi. Her favorite flower is the tulip, specifically yellow.

DANIEL W.K. LEE is a New York City-based writer whose work has been published in various online and print journals and anthologies. Favorite and influential LGBT poets and novelists include Agha Shahid Ali, Scott Hightower, Brian Leung and Tomas Mournian. His favorite flower is a tight race between the lotus and the calla lily. He can be contacted at daniel@danielextra.net.

CHIP LIVINGSTON is the author of two poetry collections *Museum of False Starts* (Gival Press, 2010) and *Crow-Blue, Crow-Black* (NYQ Books, May 2012). Recent publications include *The Florida Review, New American Writing*, and *Court Green*. Tim Dlugos and Aaron

Smith are his favorite gay writers. Iris is his favorite flower. Chip lives in Montevideo, Uruguay. His web site is www.chiplivingston.com.

BO McGUIRE hails from Hokes Bluff, Alabama. Currently, he makes catfish lipstick shine on film in New York City. His other work can be found on stages like *Lana Turner, Forklift, Ohio* and *Court Green.* He'd like to thank Dolly Parton. He's thought calla lilies the prettiest flower ever since Sister Casie marched in wearing them to senior prom.

MICHAEL MONTLACK is the author of the poetry collection *Cool Limbo* (NYQ Books, 2011) and three chapbooks, including his most recent *The Slip* (Poets Wear Prada, 2009). He is also the editor of the Lambda-Finalist essay anthology *My Diva: 65 Gay Men on the Women Who Inspire Them* (University of Wisconsin Press, 2009). He splits his time between New York City, where he teaches at Berkeley College, and San Francisco. Favorite queer authors: Gertrude Stein, Ed Field and Elizabeth Bishop. Favorite flowers: giant sunflowers that tower above him.

MIGUEL MURPHY is the author of the collection of poems, *A Book Called Rats* (Eastern Washington University Press). "My favorite flower: Orange blossoms on the Clock Vine. Reading? Susan McCabe *Descartes' Nightmare*, Manuel Puig's *The Buenos Aires Affair*, Rigoberto Gonzalez's *Black Blossoms.*"

ROBBY NADLER, a baker from Missoula, MT, is currently on bread sabbatical in Israel in conjunction with a Fulbright. Frank O'Hara visits his dreams and makes fun of his accent, but sometimes they make out with tongue. As for living writers, Eileen Myles, Ronaldo Wilson, Richard Siken, and Jamie O'Neil are close friends, though the latter three don't know that. If he could be a flower, he'd be an orange arum lily with a diet coke.

YINKA ROSE REED-NOLAN is a MFA student at California State University Fresno, where she teaches undergraduate writing and works as an editorial assistant for *The Normal School*. In her spare time she enjoys rooting for the San Francisco Giants and reading works by Dorothy Allison, Miranda July and Cherrie Moraga. You can find her other work recently featured on PANK's blog and forthcoming in the online literary journal *Niche*. Despite her middle name, daisies are her favorite flower.

ERIN ROTH recently began her adult life and is hoping she doesn't have to grow up anytime soon. She admires Alison Bechdel and David Sedaris and fondly remembers the smell of her grandmother's lily-of-the-valley growing in the back garden.

ERIC SASSON's story collection, *Margins of Tolerance*, is forthcoming from Livingston Press in May 2012. His stories have appeared in T*he Puritan, The Nashville Review, Alligator Juniper, Trans, The Ledge, MARY* magazine and *THE2NDHAND*, among others. He lives in Brooklyn, NY. "Is it okay to like flowers simply because of their names? If so, I adore hyacinths and rhododendrons. Otherwise I'm partial to white lilies. As for gay authors, I'm quite fond of the usual suspects, such as Dorothy Allison, Michael Cunningham, Alan Hollinghurst and Edmund White. Someone new whose book I loved is Justin Torres. His novel *We The Animals* is fantastic." www.ericsassonnow.com

MAUREEN SEATON has authored fifteen poetry collections, solo and collaborative—most recently, *Stealth*, with Samuel Ace (Chax Press, 2011); and *Sinéad O'Connor and Her Coat of a Thousand Bluebirds*, with Neil de la Flor (Sentence Book Award, Firewheel Editions, 2011). "I'm reading Eileen Myles again all the way through, and I just shared Stacey Waite's poems with my students in our inaugural Introduction to LGBTQ course at the University of Miami, where gardenias grow wild—yum!" www.maureenseaton.com

ELAINE SEXTON is the author of two collections of poetry, *Sleuth* and *Causeway*, both with New Issues Press. Her poems, reviews, and essays have appeared in numerous journals including *American Poetry Review*, *Art in America*, *Poetry*, and *O! the Oprah* magazine. Favorite LGBT authors reading this year: Mary Cappello, Sarah Van Arsdale, Chris Bram, Michael Sledge, Skip Wachsberger. Favorite flower: peony.

DAVID TRINIDAD's most recent book is *Dear Prudence: New and Selected Poems* (Turtle Point Press, 2011). His other books include *The Late Show* (2007), *By Myself* (with D.A. Powell, 2009), and *Plasticville* (2000), all published by Turtle Point. He is also the editor of *A Fast Life: The Collected Poems of Tim Dlugos* (Nightboat Books, 2011). Trinidad teaches poetry at Columbia College Chicago, where he co-edits the journal *Court Green*. He is currently interested in the paintings of Paul Cadmus and George Tooker. His favorite flowers are Plathian: tulips, daffodils, narcissi.

STACEY WAITE is Assistant Professor of English at the University of Nebraska–Lincoln. Waite has published three chapbooks of poems: *Choke* (2004 Frank O'Hara Prize winner) *Love Poem to Androgyny* (2006), and *the lake has no saint* (2008 Snowbound Prize winner from Tupelo Press). Waite's newest collection, *Butch Geography*, is forthcoming from Tupelo Press in 2013. This year s/he received a copy of Qwo-Li Driskill's *Walking with Ghosts* as a birthday gift. Gift indeed. As for flowers: always the orchid, because s/he enjoys a high maintenance flower, one you really have to remember to keep alive.

PHILLIP B. WILLIAMS is a Chicago native and a Cave Canem fellow. His work is published or forthcoming in *Callaloo*, *Sou'wester*, *Painted Bride Quarterly*, *Gertrude*, and others. He is currently the Poetry Editor of the online literary journal Vinyl Poetry and an HIV Tester and Prevention Counselor for Chicago House and Social Services through AIDS United's AmeriCorps program.

STEPHEN ZERENCE is an MFA candidate at American University. He is also the poetry editor of *Folio*. His favorite authors include Edmund White and James White. His favorite flower is the lotus.